# Buckle Down™

# Ohio Mathematics

## Level 8

## 2nd Edition

This book belongs to: _____

### Buckle Down
Publishing

A Haights Cross Communications Company

*Helping your schoolhouse meet the standards of the statehouse™*

ISBN 0-7836-4889-8

Catalog #2BDOH08MM01

4 5 6 7 8 9 10

Senior Editor: Paul Meyers; Project Editor: Lynn Tauro; Editor: Andrea Berger; Production Editor: Michael Hankes; Cover design: Christina Nantz; Production Director: Jennifer Booth; Art Director: Chris Wolf; Graphic Designer: Spike Schabacker; Composition: Wyndham Books.

Cover image: © Comstock Images/Jupiterimages

# TABLE OF CONTENTS

**Table of Contents**

**To the Teacher:**

"Achievement Coverage" codes are listed for each lesson in the table of contents and for each page in the shaded gray bar that runs across the top of the page in the workbook (see example to the right). These codes indicate which Ohio Objectives are covered in a given lesson or on a given page.

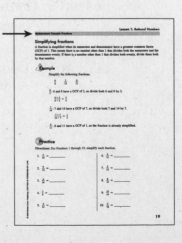

# Introduction

Not a day goes by when you don't use your math skills in some way. You use math to figure out when to wake up in the morning so you can get to school on time, to decide whether you have enough money to buy a new CD, and to estimate how much tape is needed to fix a torn book cover. You also use math when you check the temperature on a thermometer to decide whether you need to wear a jacket and when you compare the amount of time you studied for a test to your score on the test.

This book will help you practice these and many other math skills that you can use in your everyday life, as well as in school. As with anything else, the more you practice these skills, the better you will get at applying them.

# Test-Taking Tips

Here are a few general tips to keep in mind when taking any math test.

## TIP 1: On test day, stay relaxed and confident.

Before you take a test, remind yourself that you are well prepared and are going to do well. Don't let yourself become anxious. If you feel anxious before or during a test, take a couple of slow, deep breaths to relax.

## TIP 2: Work the easy questions first.

When you receive a test, quickly flip through it. Then, start with the easy questions and save the more difficult questions for the end. Before you hand in the test, flip through it again to make sure you have answered all the questions.

## TIP 3: Know when to guess.

If you aren't sure of the answer to a multiple-choice question, eliminate any answers you know are wrong, then choose the best answer remaining. Your first choice is often correct, so only change your answers if you are sure of the correction.

## TIP 4: Check your work.

Check your answers for careless mistakes. Match your actual answers against quick estimates for each problem to make sure your answers are reasonable.

## TIP 5: Answer open-ended items completely.

When answering short-answer and extended-response items, show all of your work to receive as many points as possible. Write neatly enough that your calculations will be easy to follow. Make your answer easy to see by circling it.

## TIP 6: Use all the test time given.

Use all the time that you have to work on the test. Do not stop working until the teacher tells you to. If you finish early, go back and check all your answers.

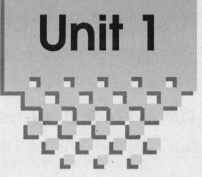

# Unit 1

# Number, Number Sense, and Operations

Did you know the Galápagos tortoise can weigh more than 500 pounds and live close to 200 years? And did you know that Mongolia—a country that's about $14\frac{3}{4}$ times the size of Ohio—has a population that is about $8.7 \cdot 10^6$ less than the population of Ohio? These facts all require you to use your understanding of numbers.

In this unit, you will review number concepts such as square roots and scientific notation. You will use your number sense to compute with different forms of rational numbers. You will also review concepts of number theory and problem solving. Finally, you will solve problems involving proportional relationships.

## In This Unit

Number Concepts

Computation and Problem Solving

Ratio and Proportion

# Lesson 1: Number Concepts

In this lesson, you will review the subsets that make up the real number system. You will also find square roots and write numbers using scientific notation.

## The Real Number System

The **real number system** consists of many different subsets.

**Whole numbers** consist of the natural numbers {1, 2, 3, . . .} and zero.

   {0, 1, 2, 3, 4, 5, . . .}

**Integers** consist of the natural numbers, their opposites, and zero.

   {. . . , −3, −2, −1, 0, 1, 2, 3, . . .}

**Rational numbers** consist of the integers and the non-integers (terminating and repeating decimals). A rational number can also be expressed as the quotient of integers (fractional form). Here are some examples:

$$\frac{2}{1} = 2 \qquad -\frac{13}{4} = -3\frac{1}{4} \qquad \frac{25}{100} = 0.25 \qquad \frac{1}{3} = 0.\overline{3}$$

**Irrational numbers** consist of numbers that **cannot** be expressed as the quotient of two integers. In decimal form, irrational numbers have neither terminating nor repeating decimals. The most common irrational number in math is **pi ($\pi$)**. The value of $\pi$ is approximately 3.14.

**Real numbers** consist of all the rational and irrational numbers. Start at the top of the tree diagram and work your way down to understand the different subsets of the real number system.

## Practice

**Directions:** For Numbers 1 through 7, write whether each real number is rational or irrational.

1. $\frac{1}{9}$ _____

2. $\sqrt{11}$ _____

3. 21.09 _____

4. −18 _____

5. $\sqrt{300}$ _____

6. $\frac{8}{17}$ _____

7. 52.7246. . . _____

8. Circle all the real numbers below that are rational.

   $-\frac{3}{4}$    0.23    17.27341. . .    7.2    $\sqrt{17}$

9. Circle all the real numbers below that are **not** integers.

   −7    0    $\frac{13}{50}$    78.3    3,416

10. Which number is rational but **not** an integer?

    A. $\sqrt{9}$

    B. $\frac{14}{7}$

    C. $\pi$

    D. $\frac{3}{5}$

11. Which real number is an integer but **not** a whole number?

    A. 12

    B. −9

    C. −3.2

    D. $\sqrt{15}$

# Square Roots

The symbol $\sqrt{\phantom{a}}$ is called a **radical sign** and indicates a **root**. For example, $\sqrt{a}$ is read "the square root of $a$." The number under the radical sign is called the **radicand**. The square root of a number is the number that, when multiplied by itself, is equal to the radicand.

Square roots are sometimes written like this: $\sqrt{144} = \pm12$. The right side of this equation includes both the positive and the negative square roots of 144; this is read "plus or minus twelve."

▷ **Example**

Since $12^2 = 12 \cdot 12 = 144$   and   $(-12)^2 = (-12) \cdot (-12) = 144$, then $\sqrt{144} = \pm12$.

**Perfect squares** have square roots that are integers. The first six perfect squares are 1, 4, 9, 16, 25, and 36.

▷ **Examples**

$\sqrt{1} = \pm1$          $\sqrt{16} = \pm4$

$\sqrt{4} = \pm2$          $\sqrt{25} = \pm5$

$\sqrt{9} = \pm3$          $\sqrt{36} = \pm6$

**Non-perfect squares** such as 2 and 5 have square roots that are irrational numbers. There are no rational numbers that, when multiplied by themselves, equal either 2 or 5. You can use a calculator to find a rational estimate of an irrational number in most problem-solving situations.

▷ **Examples**

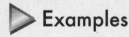

$\sqrt{2} = 1.4142135623\ldots \approx \pm1.4$      (rounded to the nearest tenth)

$\sqrt{5} = 2.2360679774\ldots \approx \pm2.2$      (rounded to the nearest tenth)

You have seen that the square root of a number can be either positive or negative. Throughout the rest of this lesson, you will write only the positive square roots of numbers.

You can estimate the square root of a number between two consecutive integers. The estimate will be between the square roots of the nearest perfect squares above and below the number for which you want to find the square root.

▷ Example

Between which two consecutive integers is the value of $\sqrt{70}$?

Since 70 is between the perfect squares 64 and 81, $\sqrt{70}$ is between $\sqrt{64}$ and $\sqrt{81}$.

$$\sqrt{64} = 8 \qquad\qquad \sqrt{81} = 9$$

The value of $\sqrt{70}$ is between 8 and 9.

● Practice

**Directions:** For Numbers 1 through 7, find each square root.

1. $\sqrt{49}$ _____

2. $\sqrt{121}$ _____

3. $\sqrt{256}$ _____

4. $\sqrt{81}$ _____

5. $\sqrt{400}$ _____

6. $\sqrt{225}$ _____

7. $\sqrt{324}$ _____

**Directions:** For Numbers 8 through 13, find the two consecutive integers between which each square root lies. Then, use a calculator to find the square root to the nearest tenth.

8. $\sqrt{35}$ _____

9. $\sqrt{7}$ _____

10. $\sqrt{21}$ _____

11. $\sqrt{45}$ _____

12. $\sqrt{110}$ _____

13. $\sqrt{222}$ _____

# Scientific Notation

**Scientific notation** is used to represent very large or very small numbers. The following table shows the first five positive and negative powers of 10.

| Powers of 10 | |
|---|---|
| **Positive** | **Negative** |
| $10^1 = 10$ | $10^{-1} = 0.1$ |
| $10^2 = 100$ | $10^{-2} = 0.01$ |
| $10^3 = 1,000$ | $10^{-3} = 0.001$ |
| $10^4 = 10,000$ | $10^{-4} = 0.0001$ |
| $10^5 = 100,000$ | $10^{-5} = 0.00001$ |
| and so on . . . | and so on . . . |

## Changing from standard form to scientific notation

A number is written in scientific notation as the product of a number greater than or equal to 1 but less than 10, the **coefficient**, and some power of 10. Follow these steps to change a number from standard form to scientific notation.

Step 1: **Move the decimal point to the *left* or *right* until you have a number greater than or equal to 1 but less than 10.**

Step 2: **Count the number of places you moved the decimal point to the *left* or *right* and use that number as the *positive* or *negative* power of 10.**

Step 3: **Multiply the decimal (in Step 1) by the power of 10 (in Step 2).**

▶ Example

Write 7,427,000 in scientific notation.

Move the decimal point 6 places to the left.

7.427000.

Since the decimal point moved 6 places to the left, multiply by $10^6$.

$7.427 \cdot 10^6$

$7,427,000 = 7.427 \cdot 10^6$

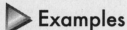 **Example**

Write 0.000237 in scientific notation.

Move the decimal point 4 places to the right.

0.0002.37

Since the decimal point moved 4 places to the right, multiply by $10^{-4}$.

$2.37 \cdot 10^{-4}$

$0.000237 = 2.37 \cdot 10^{-4}$

## Changing from scientific notation to standard form

To change a number written in scientific notation with a **positive power of 10** to standard form, move the decimal point to the **right**. The exponent shows the number of places the decimal point will be moved.

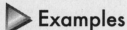 **Examples**

$3.009 \cdot 10^6 = 3.009000. = 3,009,000$

$8.462 \cdot 10^8 = 8.46200000. = 846,200,000$

To change a number written in scientific notation with a **negative power of 10** to standard form, move the decimal point to the **left**. The exponent shows the number of places the decimal point will be moved.

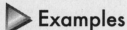 **Examples**

$7.285 \cdot 10^{-6} = 0.000007.285 = 0.000007285$

$3.57086 \cdot 10^{-3} = 0.003.57086 = 0.00357086$

## ⬤ Practice

**Directions:** For Numbers 1 through 5, write each number in scientific notation.

1. 0.0001023 _____

2. 6,544 _____

3. 9,261.38 _____

4. 0.0000672 _____

5. 57,002 _____

**Directions:** For Numbers 6 through 10, write each number in standard form.

6. $6.5 \cdot 10^6$ _____

7. $7.941 \cdot 10^{-7}$ _____

8. $8.746 \cdot 10^7$ _____

9. $1.00527 \cdot 10^{-4}$ _____

10. $7.000003 \cdot 10^4$ _____

**Directions:** For Numbers 11 through 14, write each number in standard form or scientific notation.

11. The world's population is about 6,450,000,000. How is 6,450,000,000 written in scientific notation?

_____

12. Theo's computer can add a column of 150 numbers in $5.2 \cdot 10^{-6}$ seconds. How is $5.2 \cdot 10^{-6}$ written in standard form?

_____

13. Sound can travel through 30 cm of water in about 0.0002586 seconds. How is 0.0002586 written in scientific notation?

_____

14. Last year, over $6.17 \cdot 10^7$ people visited the most popular shopping site on the internet. How is $6.17 \cdot 10^7$ written in standard form?

_____

# Comparing numbers in scientific notation

To compare numbers written in scientific notation, first compare the powers of 10. The larger the power of 10, the larger the number. If the numbers have the same power of 10, compare the coefficients. The larger the coefficient, the larger the number.

## ▷ Example

Compare $5.62 \cdot 10^6$ and $7.39 \cdot 10^5$.

Compare the powers of 10 of the numbers.

$6 > 5$

Since $6 > 5$, the number with 6 as its power of 10 is greater than the number with 5 as its power of 10.

Therefore, $5.62 \cdot 10^6 > 7.39 \cdot 10^5$.

## ▷ Example

Compare $4.29 \cdot 10^{-3}$ and $5.38 \cdot 10^{-3}$.

First, compare the powers of 10 of the numbers.

$-3 = -3$

Since the powers of 10 are each $-3$, compare the coefficients of the numbers.

$4.29 < 5.38$

Since $4.29 < 5.38$, the number with the coefficient of 4.29 is less than the number with the coefficient of 5.38.

Therefore, $4.29 \cdot 10^{-3} < 5.38 \cdot 10^{-3}$.

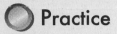 **Practice**

**Directions:** For Numbers 1 through 6, compare the numbers using <, >, or =.

1. $6.0515 \bullet 10^6$ _____ $6.12 \bullet 10^5$

2. $4.67 \bullet 10^{-3}$ _____ $3.0967 \bullet 10^{-3}$

3. $8.640 \bullet 10^8$ _____ $8.64 \bullet 10^8$

4. $5.2266 \bullet 10^{-7}$ _____ $6.025 \bullet 10^2$

5. $6.93 \bullet 10^5$ _____ $6.93 \bullet 10^{-5}$

6. $7.35 \bullet 10^{-6}$ _____ $7.305 \bullet 10^{-6}$

7. Which is heavier, a grasshopper that weighs $3.3 \bullet 10^{-3}$ pounds or a ladybug that weighs $7.03 \bullet 10^{-5}$ pounds?

_____

8. The following table shows the highest points of elevation in six U.S. states.

### States' Highest Points

| State | Altitude (in ft) |
| --- | --- |
| Hawaii | $1.3796 \bullet 10^4$ |
| Utah | $1.3528 \bullet 10^4$ |
| Oklahoma | $4.973 \bullet 10^3$ |
| Wyoming | $1.3804 \bullet 10^4$ |
| Alaska | $2.032 \bullet 10^4$ |
| Ohio | $1.549 \bullet 10^3$ |

Write the states in order from **lowest** to **highest** point of elevation.

_____

_____

# Achievement Practice

1. The mean radius of the planet Mercury is about 8,010,000 feet. How is this number written in scientific notation?

   A. $0.801 \cdot 10^7$

   B. $8.01 \cdot 10^6$

   C. $80.1 \cdot 10^5$

   D. $801 \cdot 10^4$

2. What is the value of $\sqrt{324}$?

   A. 14

   B. 16

   C. 18

   D. 22

3. A centimeter is about $4.09 \cdot 10^{-5}$ of a mile. How is this number written in standard form?

   A. 409,000

   B. 4.000009

   C. 0.0000409

   D. 0.00000409

4. Between which two consecutive integers is the value of $\sqrt{411}$? Explain your answer.

   _____

   _____

   _____

   _____

5.  Which real number is irrational?

    A.  $-\frac{13}{21}$

    B.  $\sqrt{9}$

    C.  $\pi$

    D.  4.06

6.  The following table lists the equatorial diameters of the nine planets.

    **Planets' Equatorial Diameters**

    | Planet | Diameter (in km) |
    |--------|------------------|
    | Mercury | $4.878 \cdot 10^3$ |
    | Venus | $1.210 \cdot 10^4$ |
    | Earth | $1.276 \cdot 10^4$ |
    | Mars | $6.787 \cdot 10^3$ |
    | Jupiter | $1.428 \cdot 10^5$ |
    | Saturn | $1.205 \cdot 10^5$ |
    | Uranus | $5.112 \cdot 10^4$ |
    | Neptune | $4.953 \cdot 10^4$ |
    | Pluto | $2.300 \cdot 10^3$ |

    Which planet has the **smallest** equatorial diameter?

    A.  Mars

    B.  Pluto

    C.  Venus

    D.  Saturn

# Lesson 2: Computation and Problem Solving

In this lesson, you will add, subtract, multiply, and divide numbers in scientific notation. You will use the correct order of operations to simplify numerical expressions. You will also estimate and use appropriate operations and number properties to solve problems.

## Scientific Notation

You can compute with numbers that are written in scientific notation.

## Addition and subtraction

In order to add or subtract numbers written in scientific notation, the powers of 10 must be the same. If they are the same, add or subtract the coefficients and leave the power of 10 the same. Check to see that the sum or difference is written in correct scientific notation.

▷ **Example**

Add: $(8.12 \cdot 10^6) + (5.74 \cdot 10^6)$

Since the powers of 10 are each 6, you can add the coefficients.

$8.12 + 5.74 = 13.86$

The power of 10 will stay 6.

$(8.12 \cdot 10^6) + (5.74 \cdot 10^6) = 13.86 \cdot 10^6$

Check to be sure the sum is written in correct scientific notation.

$13.86 \cdot 10^6 = 1.386 \cdot 10^7$

Therefore, $(8.12 \cdot 10^6) + (5.74 \cdot 10^6) = 1.386 \cdot 10^7$.

# Multiplication and division

When multiplying or dividing numbers written in scientific notation, multiply or divide the coefficients and use the following properties of exponents to determine the power of 10.

**product property of exponents:** when multiplying powers with the same base number, add the exponents and keep the base number the same

**quotient property of exponents:** when dividing powers with the same base number, subtract the exponent in the divisor from the exponent in the dividend and keep the base number the same

Check to see that the product or quotient is written in correct scientific notation.

## ▷ Example

Divide: $(3.9 \cdot 10^8) \div (6.5 \cdot 10^{-4})$

Divide the coefficients.

$3.9 \div 6.5 = 0.6$

Subtract the powers of 10.

$8 - (-4) = 12$

Check to be sure the quotient is written in correct scientific notation.

$(3.9 \cdot 10^8) \div (6.5 \cdot 10^{-4}) = 0.6 \cdot 10^{12} = 6.0 \cdot 10^{11}$

Therefore, $(3.9 \cdot 10^8) \div (6.5 \cdot 10^{-4}) = 6.0 \cdot 10^{11}$.

## ⬤ Practice

**Directions:** For Numbers 1 through 5, compute.

1. $(7.01 \cdot 10^{-5}) - (5.63 \cdot 10^{-5}) = $ _____

2. $(4.8 \cdot 10^2) \div (2.4 \cdot 10^6) = $ _____

3. $(7.792 \cdot 10^6) + (3.578 \cdot 10^6) = $ _____

4. $(6.2 \cdot 10^{-3}) \cdot (-3.17 \cdot 10^7) = $ _____

5. $(4.32 \cdot 10^{-9}) + (-6.002 \cdot 10^{-9}) = $ _____

# Order of Operations

Sometimes there may be more than one operation involved in a problem. When this is the case, follow this **order of operations**:

1. Simplify everything inside parentheses or other grouping symbols (such as brackets or absolute value signs). If there is a set of grouping symbols within another set, work your way from the inside to the outside.

2. Simplify square roots and exponents.

3. Multiply and divide in order, from left to right.

4. Add and subtract in order, from left to right.

▶ Example

Simplify: $(-8)^2 \div 4 - (-12 + 21) \cdot 3$

The first step is to simplify everything inside parentheses.

$(-8)^2 \div 4 - \mathbf{(-12 + 21)} \cdot 3$

$(-8)^2 \div 4 - \mathbf{9} \cdot 3$

The next step is to simplify any square roots and exponents.

$\mathbf{(-8)^2} \div 4 - 9 \cdot 3$

$\mathbf{64} \div 4 - 9 \cdot 3$

Now, multiply and divide in order, from left to right.

$\mathbf{64 \div 4} - 9 \cdot 3$

$\mathbf{16} - 9 \cdot 3$

$16 - \mathbf{9 \cdot 3}$

$16 - \mathbf{27}$

Finally, add and subtract in order, from left to right.

$\mathbf{16 - 27}$

$\mathbf{-11}$

The answer is $-11$.

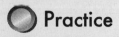 **Practice**

**Directions:** For Numbers 1 through 6, simplify.

1. $2 + 7 \cdot 2 - 3$

2. $36 - 6 \div 1 + 7.6 - 2$

3. $\sqrt{121} + 52 \div 4 \cdot 2^2$

4. $15 + (\sqrt{9} \cdot 7) \div 3$

5. $(13 - 19) \cdot (-35 + 40)$

6. $16 \cdot (4 + 5) - 21 \div \sqrt{49}$

7. Phil bought 18 golf balls and 5 bags of golf tees. A sleeve of 3 golf balls cost $2.50, and each bag of golf tees cost $1.10. The following expression represents his total cost.

    $(18 \div 3) \cdot 2.5 + 5 \cdot 1.1$

    How much did Phil spend on golf balls and golf tees? _____

# Estimation

**Rounding** is a good way to estimate the solution to a problem. The digit to be rounded will either increase by one or stay the same.

## Rounding integers and decimals

When rounding integers and decimals, remember these rules:

- Look at the digit to the **right** of the place to which you are rounding.
- If that digit is **5 or more**, the digit in the place you are rounding will increase by one. Write all the necessary digits to the right as zeros.
- If that digit is **less than 5**, the digit in the place you are rounding will stay the same. Write all the necessary digits to the right as zeros.

▶ Example

The following place-value table shows 3,189.

| Thousands | Hundreds | Tens | Ones |
|---|---|---|---|
| 3 | 1 | 8 | 9 |

Round 3,1<u>8</u>9 to the nearest ten: 3,1<u>9</u>0      (9 > 5; increase by 1)

Round 3,<u>1</u>89 to the nearest hundred: 3,<u>2</u>00      (8 > 5; increase by 1)

Round <u>3</u>,189 to the nearest thousand: <u>3</u>,000      (1 < 5; leave the same)

▶ Example

The following place-value table shows 4.235.

| Ones | | Tenths | Hundredths | Thousandths |
|---|---|---|---|---|
| 4 | . | 2 | 3 | 5 |

Round <u>4</u>.235 to the nearest whole number: <u>4</u>      (2 < 5; leave the same)

Round 4.<u>2</u>35 to the nearest tenth: 4.<u>2</u>      (3 < 5; leave the same)

Round 4.2<u>3</u>5 to the nearest hundredth: 4.2<u>4</u>      (5 = 5; increase by 1)

## ● Practice

**Directions:** For Numbers 1 through 6, round 2,954.837 to the nearest given place value.

1. thousand _____

2. hundred _____

3. ten _____

4. whole number _____

5. tenth _____

6. hundredth _____

**Directions:** Use these monthly snowfall totals to answer Numbers 7 and 8.

| December | January | February | March | April |
|----------|---------|----------|-------|-------|
| 3.25 in. | 7.625 in. | 6.028 in. | 2.95 in. | 0.75 in. |

7. Use rounding to estimate the total amount of snow to the nearest inch for the five months given.

_____

8. Compute the total amount of snow for the five months given. _____

9. One bottle of water and a small bag of crackers cost $2.18 at the store. If Jill is buying one of each item for 14 people, **about** how much money will she spend?

   A. $24

   B. $27

   C. $29

   D. $32

10. Three items cost $12.15, $11.95, and $18.49. **About** how much money is needed to buy all three items?

    A. $40

    B. $45

    C. $50

    D. $55

# Rounding fractions and mixed numbers

When rounding a fraction to the nearest whole number, it is usually part of a mixed number. When the fraction part is $\frac{1}{2}$ **or greater**, drop the fraction and increase the whole number by one. When the fraction part is **less than** $\frac{1}{2}$, drop the fraction and leave the whole number the same.

## ▷ Example

Round $5\frac{3}{10}$ to the nearest whole number.

The fraction $\frac{3}{10}$ is less than $\frac{1}{2}$, so drop the fraction and leave the whole number the same. The answer is 5.

## ▷ Example

Round $21\frac{4}{7}$ to the nearest whole number.

The fraction $\frac{4}{7}$ is greater than $\frac{1}{2}$, so drop the fraction and increase the whole number by one. The answer is 22.

## ◯ Practice

**Directions:** For Numbers 1 through 5, round to the nearest whole number.

1. $33\frac{8}{13}$ _____

2. $17\frac{7}{9}$ _____

3. $2\frac{2}{5}$ _____

4. $41\frac{8}{19}$ _____

5. $16\frac{1}{2}$ _____

6. What is $15\frac{6}{11}$ rounded to the nearest whole number?

A. 14
B. 15
C. 16
D. 20

7. What is $22\frac{7}{8}$ rounded to the nearest whole number?

A. 20
B. 22
C. 23
D. 24

# Number Properties

A **number property** states a relationship between numbers. The following are two number properties that you probably already use without even realizing it.

## Identity properties

Identity properties show what happens when you add zero to a number or multiply a number by one.

The **identity property of addition** states that zero added to a number is equal to that same number.

$$a + 0 = a \qquad\qquad 19 + 0 = 19$$

The **identity property of multiplication** states that a number multiplied by one is equal to that same number.

$$a \cdot 1 = a \qquad\qquad 13 \cdot 1 = 13$$

## Inverse properties

Inverse properties show what happens when you add a number's opposite to that number or multiply a number by its reciprocal.

The **inverse property of addition** states that a number added to its opposite is equal to zero.

$$a + (-a) = 0 \qquad\qquad 7 + (-7) = 0$$

The **inverse property of multiplication** states that a number multiplied by its reciprocal is equal to one.

$$\frac{a}{b} \cdot \frac{b}{a} = 1 \qquad\qquad \frac{7}{8} \cdot \frac{8}{7} = 1$$

# ⬤ Practice

**Directions:** For Numbers 1 through 4, write the number property that each example represents.

1. $-\frac{2}{3} + \frac{2}{3} = 0$ _____

2. $452 + 0 = 452$ _____

3. $\frac{2}{3} \cdot \frac{3}{2} = 1$ _____

4. $1 \cdot 55 = 55$ _____

**Directions:** For Numbers 5 through 8, compute using the identity and inverse properties of addition and multiplication.

5. $12 \cdot \frac{1}{12} \cdot 7 = $ _____

6. $27 + (-32) + 32 = $ _____

7. $(74 - 74) + (-53 + 53) = $ _____

8. $54 \cdot (12 \div 12) = $ _____

9. Explain how you can use the identity and inverse properties of addition to find the following sum in your head.

$$15{,}827 + (-15{,}827) + 53{,}904$$

_____

_____

_____

_____

# Achievement Practice

1. Simplify the following expression.

    $$-32 \div 8 + 2^3 \bullet (-3 - 3)$$

    A.  12

    B.  0

    C.  24

    D.  -52

2. Pat went on vacation last week. The following table shows how much money she spent each day of her vacation.

### Pat's Vacation Spendings

| Day | Amount Spent |
|-----------|--------------|
| Monday | $26.15 |
| Tuesday | $25.85 |
| Wednesday | $37.28 |
| Thursday | $45.54 |
| Friday | $17.52 |

What is the total amount of money Pat spent during the entire week?

    A.  $152.34

    B.  $152.64

    C.  $153.34

    D.  $153.64

3. Marty went shopping and spent $15.85 on a pair of sunglasses, $23.19 on a shirt, and $7.84 on socks. Then, he spent $6.69 on lunch. **About** how much money did Marty spend altogether?

   A. $56

   B. $54

   C. $52

   D. $50

4. What is 3,518.477 rounded to the nearest hundred?

   A. 3,500

   B. 3,518.48

   C. 3,600

   D. 3,600.47

5. The population of Asia is about $3.9 \cdot 10^9$. The population of Europe is about $7.3 \cdot 10^8$. The population of Africa is about $8.9 \cdot 10^7$. The combined population for the remaining continents is about $3.3 \cdot 10^7$. **About** how many more people live in Asia than the other continents of the world?

   A. $3.05 \cdot 10^8$

   B. $1.95 \cdot 10^8$

   C. $3.048 \cdot 10^9$

   D. $3.5 \cdot 10^9$

6. What number property does the following example represent?

   $-13.2 + 13.2 = 0$

   _____

**25**

# Lesson 3: Ratio and Proportion

In this lesson, you will review proportional relationships and find solutions to application problems involving proportions and percents.

## Ratio

A **ratio** is a comparison of two numbers. In this lesson, you will write ratios as reduced fractions. If a ratio is an improper fraction, it is left as an improper fraction and **not** written as a mixed number.

▷ Example

Seven teachers from Roy Rogers High School were chaperones at a school dance. There were two math teachers, three English teachers, one science teacher, and one art teacher. What is the ratio of English teacher chaperones to all teacher chaperones?

$$\frac{\text{English teacher chaperones}}{\text{all teacher chaperones}} = \frac{3}{7}$$

The ratio of English teacher chaperones to all teacher chaperones is $\frac{3}{7}$.

◯ Practice

**Directions:** Use the following information to answer Numbers 1 through 4.

During one game, a football team played 45 minutes on defense and 15 minutes on offense.

1. What is the ratio of minutes on defense to minutes on offense? _____

2. What is the ratio of minutes on offense to minutes on defense? _____

3. What is the ratio of minutes on offense to the total number of minutes in the game?

   _____

4. What is the ratio of minutes on defense to the total number of minutes in the game?

   _____

**26**

# Proportion

A **proportion** states that two ratios are equal. A proportion has two **cross products** that are equal to each other.

▷ **Example**

Verify that $\frac{3}{5} = \frac{6}{10}$ is a proportion by multiplying diagonally to find the cross products.

$$\frac{3}{5} \times \frac{6}{10}$$

$$3 \cdot 10 = 5 \cdot 6$$

$$30 = 30$$

Since the equation is true, the proportion is also true.

▷ **Example**

Is the relationship between the number of eggs and the total cost proportional?

| Number of Eggs | Total Cost |
| --- | --- |
| 12 | $1.50 |
| 24 | $3.00 |
| 36 | $4.50 |

Set up a proportion between the information in the first and second rows and also in the second and third rows. Then, find the cross products.

$$\frac{12}{24} = \frac{1.50}{3.00} \qquad\qquad \frac{24}{36} = \frac{3.00}{4.50}$$

$$12 \cdot 3.00 = 24 \cdot 1.50 \qquad 24 \cdot 4.50 = 36 \cdot 3.00$$

$$36.00 = 36.00 \qquad\qquad 108.00 = 108.00$$

The cross products between the information in the first and second rows are equal. The cross products between the information in the second and third rows are also equal. Therefore, there is a proportional relationship between the number of eggs and the total cost.

## Practice

**Directions:** For Numbers 1 through 8, use cross products to determine whether the proportion is true or false.

1. $\frac{7}{14} = \frac{13}{26}$ _____

2. $\frac{28}{42} = \frac{2}{3}$ _____

3. $\frac{3}{9} = \frac{81}{135}$ _____

4. $\frac{5}{7} = \frac{80}{112}$ _____

5. $\frac{21}{56} = \frac{42}{98}$ _____

6. $\frac{8}{24} = \frac{17}{51}$ _____

7. $\frac{13}{24} = \frac{65}{120}$ _____

8. $\frac{6}{12} = \frac{24}{50}$ _____

**Directions:** Use proportions to answer Numbers 9 and 10.

9. Is the relationship between the number of bricks and the total weight proportional?

_____

| Number of Bricks | Weight (in lbs) |
|---|---|
| 10 | 32 |
| 45 | 144 |
| 80 | 256 |

10. Is the relationship between the capacity and the number of servings proportional?

_____

| Capacity (in mL) | Number of Servings |
|---|---|
| 250 | 1 |
| 1,000 | 4 |
| 2,000 | 6 |

**28**

# Percent

When you want to find a missing percent, set up a proportion and solve. A percent can be written as a fraction with a denominator of 100.

▷ **Example**

What percent of 25 is 5?

Set up a proportion. Let $n$ = the percent.

$$\frac{5}{25} = \frac{n}{100}$$

Cross multiply and solve.

$25n = 5 \cdot 100$      $(25n = 25 \cdot n)$

$25n = 500$      (Divide both sides by 25.)

$n = 20$

5 is 20% of 25.

You can also use proportions to solve real-world problems involving percents.

▷ **Example**

Joanne's family went out to dinner. The bill for the meal was $62. Joanne's dad left a 15% tip. What was the amount of the tip?

Set up a proportion. Let $t$ = amount of the tip.

$$\frac{t}{62} = \frac{15}{100}$$

Cross multiply and solve.

$100t = 62 \cdot 15$

$100t = 930$

$t = 9.3$

The amount of the tip was $9.30.

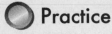 **Practice**

1.  What percent of 45 is 18? _____

2.  17 is 85% of what number? _____

3.  70 is what percent of 125? _____

4.  What number is 60% of 52? _____

**Directions:** For Numbers 5 through 8, first estimate an answer. Then, use proportions to find the exact answer.

5.  This season, Lindsey hit 150% of the number of home runs that she hit last season. If she hit 12 home runs last season, how many home runs did Lindsey hit this season?

    estimate _____

    actual _____

6.  Nick and Nora ordered two chicken sandwiches that cost $6.95 each and two lemonades that cost $1.85 each. The total cost included a sales tax of 5.75%. They left 15% of the total cost for a tip. How much did Nick and Nora pay altogether?

    estimate _____

    actual _____

7.  Sally received a bonus that was 30% of her monthly earnings. If her monthly earnings were $930, how much was Sally's bonus?

    estimate _____

    actual _____

8.  Jesse read in a textbook that the human body, by mass, is made up of 1.5% calcium. If Jesse weighs 160 pounds, how many pounds of his body mass are calcium?

    estimate _____

    actual _____

# Rate

A **rate** is a fixed ratio between two quantities. You can use proportions to solve problems involving rates.

## ▷ Example

An SUV will travel 35 miles on 2.5 gallons of gasoline. How far will the SUV travel on 25 gallons of gasoline?

Set up a proportion. Let $x$ = the distance traveled on 25 gallons of gasoline.

$$\frac{35 \text{ miles}}{2.5 \text{ gallons}} = \frac{x}{25 \text{ gallons}}$$

Cross multiply and solve.

$$2.5x = 35 \cdot 25$$
$$2.5x = 875$$
$$x = 350$$

The SUV will travel 350 miles on 25 gallons of gasoline.

## ▷ Example

At a butcher's counter, the unit cost for ground beef is $2.59 per pound. What will be the cost for 5 pounds of ground beef?

Since you are given the unit cost, you simply need to multiply the unit cost (a constant factor) by the number of pounds of ground beef. Let $c$ = the cost for 5 pounds of ground beef.

$$c = 2.59 \cdot 5$$
$$= 12.95$$

The cost for 5 pounds of ground beef will be $12.95.

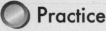 **Practice**

1. A train traveled 245 miles in 4 hours and 43 minutes. **Estimate** the distance traveled by the train in one hour.

   _____

2. A plastic injection machine can make 18 plastic wheels in one minute. How many wheels can it make in 25 minutes?

   _____

3. Clint's Crazy Bargains is selling pencils for $0.85 each. How much will one dozen pencils cost?

   _____

4. Harriet drove for 3 hours and 42 minutes from Dayton to Marietta at an average rate of 53 miles per hour. **Estimate** the distance Harriet traveled.

   _____

5. Madeline runs 3 miles in 16 minutes. Assuming that she keeps up the same pace, how long will it take Madeline to run 7 miles? Round you answer to the nearest minute.

   _____

6. Sophie drove 556 kilometers in 8 hours. At this rate, **estimate** how many hours it will take Sophie to drive 900 kilometers.

   _____

7. Audrey read 32 pages in 1 hour and 12 minutes. At this rate, **estimate** how long it will take Audrey to read a book of 270 pages.

   _____

8. Donald earned $285 for almost 40 hours of work. **Estimate** Donald's hourly wage.

   _____

# Achievement Practice

1. Which proportion is true?

   A. $\dfrac{9}{14} = \dfrac{81}{140}$

   B. $\dfrac{17}{35} = \dfrac{18}{37}$

   C. $\dfrac{13}{65} = \dfrac{24}{120}$

   D. $\dfrac{12}{72} = \dfrac{20}{150}$

2. A bookstore sold 75,000 books last year. Of the books sold, 11,500 were autobiographies. What percent of the books sold were autobiographies?

   A. 10%

   B. 15%

   C. 20%

   D. 25%

3. There are 32 players on the coed soccer team. Eighteen of them are boys and the rest are girls. What is the ratio of girls to boys?

   A. $\dfrac{14}{32}$

   B. $\dfrac{18}{32}$

   C. $\dfrac{14}{18}$

   D. $\dfrac{18}{14}$

4. Keenan saved $60 to buy a new bike. The bike he is going to buy costs 550% of the amount he has saved. How much does the bike cost?

   A. $240

   B. $270

   C. $300

   D. $330

5. Dorothy can cross-country ski 2 miles in 13 minutes. At that rate, how long will it take Dorothy to ski 7 miles?

   A.  6 minutes

   B. 19.5 minutes

   C. 42 minutes

   D. 45.5 minutes

6. Tim intercepted a total of 3 passes in the first two football games this season. If he keeps this pace, how many passes will Tim intercept after 15 games? Set up and solve a proportion. Round your answer to the nearest whole number.

   _____

7. A dealership sold motorcycles in two colors last week: 42 black and 24 red. What is the ratio of red to black motorcycles?

   A. $\frac{42}{24}$

   B. $\frac{4}{7}$

   C. $\frac{12}{21}$

   D. $\frac{14}{8}$

8. Aubree is checking the mileage on her new car. She has driven 147 miles and used 6.8 gallons of gasoline. **About** how many miles did Aubree average per gallon of gasoline?

   A. 17

   B. 19

   C. 21

   D. 23

9. Jim answered 4 questions incorrectly on a 25-question test. What percent of the test questions did Jim answer **correctly**?

   A. 16%

   B. 20%

   C. 80%

   D. 84%

10. Gabby traveled 155 miles in 2.5 hours. What was the average distance Gabby traveled each hour?

    A. 67 miles

    B. 65 miles

    C. 62 miles

    D. 55 miles

11. Which table does **not** represent a proportional relationship?

    A.

    | Hours Worked | Money Earned |
    |---|---|
    | 7 | $56 |
    | 12 | $96 |
    | 20 | $160 |

    B.

    | Points Scored | Fouls |
    |---|---|
    | 17 | 3 |
    | 34 | 6 |
    | 51 | 9 |

    C.

    | Height (in.) | Weight (lb) |
    |---|---|
    | 62 | 120 |
    | 64 | 150 |
    | 68 | 180 |

    D.

    | Ounces | Cost |
    |---|---|
    | 72 | $3 |
    | 144 | $6 |
    | 216 | $9 |

# Unit 2

# Patterns, Functions, and Algebra

You may be wondering how patterns, functions, and algebra can be used in the real world. They are used more often than you might think. Biologists use number patterns to analyze population growth. Phone companies use functions to determine the cost for using their long-distance service. You have probably noticed a relationship between the amount of time you study for a test and the score you receive.

In this unit, you will simplify, evaluate, and write expressions as well as write and solve simple equations and inequalities. You will graph equations and inequalities, including systems of linear equations and quadratic equations. You will differentiate and explain types of changes in mathematical relationships. Finally, you will extend sequences to find the $n$th term, compute with polynomials, and use a coordinate plane to find the slope of a line, the midpoint of a segment, and the distance between two points.

## In This Unit

Expressions, Equations, and Inequalities

Graphing Equations and Inequalities

Systems of Linear Equations

Relationships

Algebraic Concepts

# Lesson 4: Expressions, Equations, and Inequalities

In this lesson, you will simplify, evaluate, and write algebraic expressions. You will also write and solve equations and inequalities.

## Simplifying Expressions

To simplify an algebraic expression, you need to combine the **like terms**. Like terms have the same variables with the same exponents. If two terms are like terms, then only their coefficients may differ. Once you find all the like terms, you can combine them by adding or subtracting the coefficients only.

▶ **Examples**

| Expression | Combine like terms | Simplify |
|---|---|---|
| $12x - 7x + 4$ | $12x - 7x = 5x$ | $5x + 4$ |
| $6z - 21 + 13z$ | $6z + 13z = 19z$ | $19z - 21$ |
| $7y + 14 - 27$ | $14 - 27 = -13$ | $7y - 13$ |
| $x^2 + 3x^2 - 17$ | $x^2 + 3x^2 = 4x^2$ | $4x^2 - 17$ |

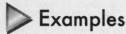 **Practice**

**Directions:** For Numbers 1 through 8, simplify the expression.

1. $9t + 5t$

2. $13 - 6x + 14$

3. $23z - 10 + 12z$

4. $6(c - 1) - 4c$

5. $-8(n + 11) + 4n$

6. $v - 17 + 4v - 8$

7. $6x + 8x - 4 + 10$

8. $3w - 9 - 6w - 5$

# Evaluating Expressions

To evaluate an expression, substitute a given value for a variable and then simplify the expression. Make sure you follow the correct order of operations.

▷ **Example**

Evaluate the following expression for $n = 30$.

$$5n - 17$$

Substitute 30 for $n$ in the expression and then simplify the expression.

$$5n - 17 = 5(\mathbf{30}) - 17$$
$$= 150 - 17$$
$$= 133$$

The answer is 133.

● **Practice**

**Directions:** For Numbers 1 through 8, evaluate each expression for the given value(s) of the variable(s).

1. $18 + 6r$ for $r = 9$

2. $-7p - 4$ for $p = -9$

3. $-10xy$ for $x = -11$ and $y = -4$

4. $5(2a + 6b)$ for $a = -12$ and $b = 4$

5. $\frac{2bc}{-3}$ for $b = 18$ and $c = 5$

6. $8(w - y)$ for $w = 2$ and $y = 11$

7. $6x - 8y$ for $x = 25$ and $y = 15$

8. $\frac{5r}{2s}$ for $r = -7$ and $s = 21$

# Writing Expressions

When an expression is written using words and phrases, you can translate it into a mathematical expression using numbers and symbols. The following list shows the operations that may be suggested by words or phrases.

**Addition:** sum, more, more than, plus, increased by, gain, exceed

**Subtraction:** difference, less, less than, minus, decreased by, diminish

**Multiplication:** product, multiplied by, of, times, twice, triple, quadruple

**Division:** quotient, divided by, ratio, half, third, fourth, per

When the operation is addition or multiplication, the order in which you write the terms **does not** matter. (The operations of addition and multiplication are **commutative**.) When the main operation is subtraction or division, the order in which you write the terms **does** matter.

## ▶ Examples

a number increased by twelve

$m + 12$ or $12 + m$

the product of five and a number

$5 \cdot x$ or $5x$

the quotient of six times a number and eleven

$6p \div 11$ or $\frac{6p}{11}$

twenty more than triple a number

$3r + 20$ or $20 + 3r$

the difference of a number and ten

$w - 10$

eight less than seven times a number

$7k - 8$

thirty-seven less than a number

$z - 37$

## ⬤ Practice

**Directions:** For Numbers 1 through 5, underline the part or parts of the phrase that indicate an operation. Then, choose a variable to represent the unknown number and write the correct expression.

1. sixteen increased by a number _____

2. a number decreased by three _____

3. an amount per fifty _____

4. the sum of seven and half a number _____

5. four more than the product of a number and six _____

**Directions:** For Numbers 6 through 9, find the error in the expression. Then, write the correct expression in the blank.

6. four more than the product of three and a number: $3(n + 4)$ _____

7. fourteen less the product of eight and a number: $8w - 14$ _____

8. the quotient of twenty-one and a number: $\frac{n}{21}$ _____

9. thirteen increased by the product of three and a number: $3y(13)$

_____

10. Which phrase is the same as the algebraic expression $4x - 25$?

   A. four times twenty-five minus a number

   B. twenty-five less than four times a number

   C. twenty-five less four times a number

   D. the difference of twenty-five and four times a number

# Applications of Expressions

You can write, simplify, and evaluate expressions to solve problems.

▷ **Example**

Write an expression that represents Olivia's age if she is four years younger than twice her sister Amy's age, $a$.

$2a - 4$

Olivia is $2a - 4$ years old.

How old is Olivia if Amy is 11 years old?

Evaluate $2a - 4$ for $a = 11$.

$$2a - 4 = 2(11) - 4$$
$$= 22 - 4$$
$$= 18$$

Olivia is 18 years old.

▷ **Example**

Write an expression that represents the sale price of an item with a retail price of $d$ dollars if there is a 15% discount in price.

$d - 0.15d$

This expression can be simplified.

$$d - 0.15d = (1 - 0.15)d$$
$$= 0.85d$$

What is the sale price of a shirt with a retail price of $36.99? Round your answer to the nearest cent.

$$0.85d = 0.85(36.99)$$
$$= 31.4415$$

The sale price of the shirt is $31.44.

## ⬤ Practice

1. Write an expression for the sum of the ages of Carol and Margie if Carol is 5 years older than Margie, $m$.

   _____

   What is the sum of the ages of Carol and Margie if Margie is 12 years old?

   _____

2. Write an expression that represents the number of goals that Heidi scored if she scored 5 less than twice as many as Josh scored, $j$.

   _____

   How many goals did Heidi score if Josh scored 29? _____

3. Write an expression that represents the area of a trapezoid if the area can be found by taking the product of 0.5, the height of the trapezoid, $h$, and the sum of the lengths of the bases, $b_1$ and $b_2$.

   _____

   What is the area of a trapezoid in $\text{ft}^2$ with a height of 12 ft and base lengths of 7 ft and 11 ft?

   _____

4. Write an expression that represents the total cost of renting a car for $22.95 per day, $d$, plus $0.08 for each mile the car is driven, $m$.

   _____

   Erin's family rented a car for 4 days and drove 212 miles. What was the total cost to rent the car?

   _____

# Solving Equations and Inequalities

An **equation** shows that two expressions are equal. An **inequality** shows that the two expressions may or may not be equal.

To solve equations, use **inverse operations** to isolate the variable on one side of the equation. Inverse operations "undo" each other. Addition and subtraction, multiplication and division, and squaring and square roots are examples of pairs of inverse operations. You can check your answer to any equation by substituting your answer into the **original equation** and simplifying.

## ▷ Example

What is the solution to the following equation?

$$4m - 44 = 46$$

Use inverse operations to solve for $m$.

$$4m - 44 = 46$$

$$4m - 44 + \mathbf{44} = 46 + \mathbf{44} \qquad \text{(Add 44 to both sides.)}$$

$$4m = 90$$

$$\frac{4m}{4} = \frac{90}{4} \qquad \text{(Divide both sides by 4.)}$$

$$m = 22.5$$

## ▷ Example

What is the solution to the following equation?

$$z^2 + 12 = 61$$

Use inverse operations to solve for $z$.

$$z^2 + 12 = 61$$

$$z^2 + 12 - \mathbf{12} = 61 - \mathbf{12} \qquad \text{(Subtract 12 from both sides.)}$$

$$z^2 = 49$$

$$\sqrt{z^2} = \sqrt{49} \qquad \text{(Take the square roots of both sides.)}$$

$$z = \pm 7 \qquad \text{(This type of problem will have two solutions.)}$$

The steps that apply to solving equations also apply to solving inequalities. Remember, if you multiply or divide both sides of an inequality by a negative number, switch the sign to the opposite direction. You can check your answer to an inequality by substituting any number in the solution into the **original equation** and simplifying.

▷ Example

What is the solution to the following inequality?

$$-5y - 4 \geq 51$$

Use inverse operations to solve for $y$.

$$-5y - 4 \geq 51$$

$$-5y - 4 + \mathbf{4} \geq 51 + \mathbf{4} \qquad \text{(Add 4 to both sides.)}$$

$$-5y \geq 55$$

$$\frac{-5y}{-5} \geq \frac{55}{-5} \qquad \text{(Divide both sides by } -5 \text{; switch the sign.)}$$

$$y \leq -11$$

▷ Example

What is the solution to the following inequality?

$$6\sqrt{k} + 25 < 73$$

Use inverse operations to solve for $k$.

$$6\sqrt{k} + 25 < 73$$

$$6\sqrt{k} + 25 - \mathbf{25} < 73 - \mathbf{25} \qquad \text{(Subtract 25 from both sides.)}$$

$$6\sqrt{k} < 48$$

$$\frac{6\sqrt{k}}{6} < \frac{48}{6} \qquad \text{(Divide both sides by 6.)}$$

$$\sqrt{k} < 8$$

$$(\sqrt{k})^2 < 8^2 \qquad \text{(Square both sides.)}$$

$$k < 64$$

## ⬤ Practice

**Directions:** For Numbers 1 through 12, solve the equation or inequality for the given variable.

1. $-6 + \frac{n}{5} \geq 0$

7. $\frac{3}{8}z - \frac{1}{4} \geq \frac{1}{2}$

2. $7t^2 - 11 = 52$

8. $20 - \frac{s}{12} = -12$

3. $4g \div 3 = -16$

9. $7\sqrt{v} + 10 \leq 80$

4. $-\frac{1}{3}y - 7 < -5$

10. $d - 34.7 = -82.6$

5. $-2\sqrt{n} + 8 \geq -6$

11. $18 - 4p^2 = -82$

6. $16 - 16k = -64$

   A. $k = 3$

   B. $k = 5$

   C. $k = -3$

   D. $k = -5$

12. $y - 21 \geq -50$

   A. $y \geq -71$

   B. $y \geq -29$

   C. $y \leq 29$

   D. $y \leq 71$

# Writing and Solving Equations and Inequalities

Sometimes you will have to write an equation to solve a real-world problem. When you read an equation in word form and then write it in number form, the word *is* means *is equal to* and is represented by an equal sign (=).

▷ **Example**

Tony has twice as many baseball cards as Jack. Together they have 105 cards. If $b$ represents the number of baseball cards that Jack has, how many cards does each boy have?

You can write the following equation and solve for $b$.

| | |
|---|---|
| $b + 2b = 105$ | ($2b$ represents the number of cards that Tony has.) |
| $3b = 105$ | (Simplify.) |
| $b = 35$ | (Divide both sides by 3.) |
| $2b = 70$ | |

Jack has 35 baseball cards and Tony has 70 baseball cards.

The steps that apply to writing equations also apply to writing inequalities. Here are a few words that usually indicate an inequality: *at least, more than, less than, no more than, greater than, no less than, minimum, maximum.*

▷ **Example**

Grace has $47 to spend at the computer store. She will buy a game for $20 and some blank CDs for $2 each. What is the maximum number of blank CDs, $c$, that Grace can buy?

You can write the following inequality and solve for $c$.

| | |
|---|---|
| $2c + 20 \leq 47$ | |
| $2c \leq 27$ | (Subtract 20 from both sides.) |
| $c \leq 13.5$ | (Divide both sides by 2.) |

The greatest whole number less than 13.5 is 13. Therefore, Grace can buy a maximum of 13 blank CDs.

## ⬤ Practice

**Directions:** For Numbers 1 through 6, write an equation or inequality and solve for the chosen variable.

1. Mrs. Mable wants to divide the students in her class into groups of no more than 3 students. If there are 34 students in the class, what is the least number of groups, $g$, into which the students can be divided?

2. The school library had a book sale and priced all books at $0.50 each. Danielle brought $3.45 to spend at the sale. What is the maximum number of books, $b$, that Danielle could have bought?

3. Admission to a theme park is $125 for the first 8 members of a group and $9 for each additional member, $m$. What is the largest group of people that can be admitted into the park for less than $190?

4. At the deli, a sub sandwich with 8 ounces of meat costs $5.35. Extra meat is available for $0.30 per ounce. If Scott bought a sub for $6.55, how much extra meat, $m$, did he order?

5. Karen's age is 7 years more than 9 times the age of her niece Emma. If the sum of their ages is 57, what is Emma's age, $e$?

6. The area of the Sternberg's patio is 85 square feet less than 4 times the area of the Moore's patio. The Sternberg's patio has an area of 526 square feet. If the Moore's patio is square, what is the side length, $s$, of the Moore's patio? (Hint: the area of a square is equal to the side length squared.) Round your answer to the nearest tenth.

# Graphing Inequalities

The graph of a simple inequality that has a sign of $<$ or $>$ will show an **open dot** at the number and part of the number line will be shaded. The number at which the open dot is located **is not** part of the solution. The graph of a simple inequality that has a sign of $\leq$ or $\geq$ will show a **closed dot** at the number and part of the number line will be shaded. The number at which the closed dot is located **is** part of the solution. The shaded part of the number line will show the numbers that can be substituted into the inequality to make the inequality true.

## ▶ Example

The following graph shows the solution to the inequality $n > 11$.

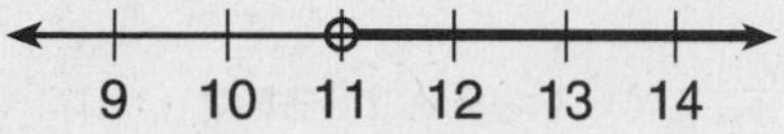

There is an open dot at 11 because of the $>$ sign. If you substitute 11 into the inequality, you will get a false inequality. The part of the number line to the right of 11 is shaded because any of these numbers can be substituted into the inequality to make it true. None of the numbers to the left of 11 will make the inequality true.

## ● Practice

**Directions:** For Numbers 1 through 6, solve the inequality and then graph the solution.

1. $12m > -72$

2. $n - 4 < 8$

3. $2n + 3 \leq 5$

4. $34 - 10z < 14$

5. $8n - 55 \geq 9$

6. $3y + 13 \leq 4$

# Achievement Practice

1. What is the solution to the following equation?

    $32 + 3n = 68$

    A. $n = 36$

    B. $n = 18$

    C. $n = 16$

    D. $n = 12$

2. Pam's summer monthly gas bill is two fifths of her winter monthly gas bill, *g*. Which expression shows the amount of Pam's summer monthly gas bill?

    A. $\frac{1}{5}g$

    B. $\frac{2}{5}g$

    C. $\frac{5}{2}g$

    D. $2g + 5$

3. Tommy's batting average is twice Walter's average, *w*. The sum of their averages is 0.546. Which equation can be used to find Tommy's batting average?

    A. $2w = 0.546$

    B. $w + 2w = 0.546$

    C. $w + \frac{1}{2}w = 0.546$

    D. $2w^2 = 0.546$

4. Simplify the following expression.

   $-5(8 - 3p) + 4p$

   A. $p - 40$

   B. $40 - 11p$

   C. $19p - 40$

   D. $-40 + 19p$

5. What is the solution to the following inequality?

   $-\dfrac{m}{2.1} > 9.47$

   A. $m > 19.887$

   B. $m > 7.37$

   C. $m < -19.887$

   D. $m < 11.57$

6. Ten less than the product of $-4$ and a number, $y$, is less than $-54$. What is the value of $y$?

   A. $y > 11$

   B. $y < -11$

   C. $y = 11$

   D. $y < 11$

7. What is the solution to the following inequality?

   $12 - 3x < -4.2$

   A. $x < 2.733$

   B. $x > -2.733$

   C. $x < -5.4$

   D. $x > 5.4$

8. Nikki spent $14 less than five times the amount Judith spent, *j*, at the store.

   Write an expression to represent the amount of money Nikki spent at the store.

   _____

9. How is "nine more than the quotient of twenty-four and a number" written as an algebraic expression?

   A. $24n + 9$

   B. $\dfrac{24}{n} + 9$

   C. $\dfrac{n}{24} + 9$

   D. $24n - 9$

10. What is the solution to the following equation?

    $$n^2 + 6 = 55$$

    A. $n = \pm 7$
    B. $n = \pm 24$
    C. $n = \pm 49$
    D. $n = \pm 2{,}401$

11. The square root of some number increased by 8 is 17. What is the number?

    A. 3
    B. 9
    C. 81
    D. 121

12. Toby has $6 to spend for lunch. He buys onion rings for $1.89 and a soda for $1.29. If he spends his remaining money on hamburgers that cost $0.98 each, what is the maximum number of hamburgers Toby can buy?

    A. 4

    B. 3

    C. 2

    D. 1

13. Which graph shows the solution to the following inequality?

    $$22x - 12 < 43$$

    A.

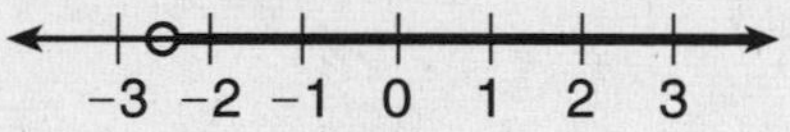

    B.

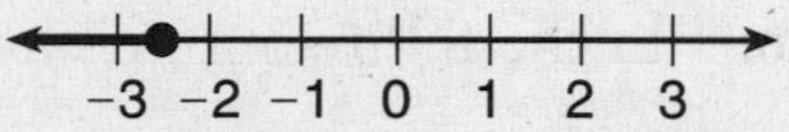

    C.

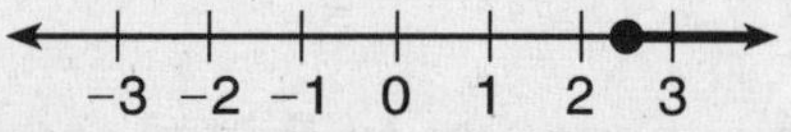

    D.

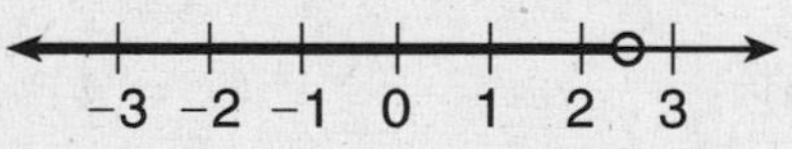

14. Evaluate the following expression for $z = -4$.

    $$2^2 \cdot (13 - 16 \div z^2) \div (-3z + 4)$$

# Lesson 5: Graphing Equations and Inequalities

In this lesson, you will graph linear equations, linear inequalities, and quadratic equations.

## Graphing Linear Equations

To find solutions to a linear equation in two variables, find a pair of numbers ($x$ and $y$) that, when substituted into the equation, make the equation true. These values of $x$ and $y$ form an ordered pair $(x, y)$. Use a table of values to generate at least three ordered pairs by choosing any arbitrary value for $x$ or $y$, substituting that value into the equation, and then solving for the other variable. The easiest values to work with are usually $x = 0$ and $y = 0$, and then some third value for either $x$ or $y$.

▷ **Example**

Find three ordered pairs that are solutions to the following linear equation.

$x + 4y = 8$

Substitute $x = 0$, $y = 0$, and $x = 4$ into the equation to find three ordered pairs.

| $(x = 0)$ | $(y = 0)$ | $(x = 4)$ |
|---|---|---|
| $x + 4y = 8$ | $x + 4y = 8$ | $x + 4y = 8$ |
| $0 + 4y = 8$ | $x + 4(0) = 8$ | $4 + 4y = 8$ |
| $4y = 8$ | $x + 0 = 8$ | $4y = 4$ |
| $y = 2$ | $x = 8$ | $y = 1$ |

Write these values into a table and find the ordered pairs.

| x | y |
|---|---|
| 0 | 2 |
| 8 | 0 |
| 4 | 1 |

Three ordered pairs that are solutions to the equation are $(0, 2)$, $(8, 0)$, and $(4, 1)$.

After you have found a few solutions to a linear equation, you can graph the solutions on the coordinate plane. Use the ordered pairs to plot the points on the graph, and then connect the points to form a line. The line represents **all** the solutions to the linear equation.

## ▷ Example

Using the ordered pairs you found in the previous example, graph the equation $x + 4y = 8$. The ordered pairs are (0, 2), (8, 0), and (4, 1).

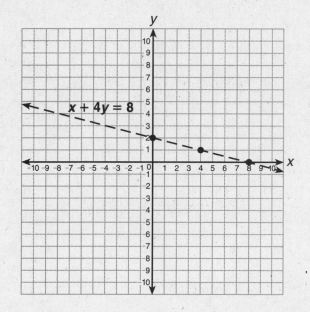

The ordered pairs (0, 2), (8, 0), and (4, 1) are only three solutions to the equation $x + 4y = 8$. There is an infinite number of solutions that can be represented by the ordered pairs for every point on the line.

In the example, the points (8, 0) and (0, 2) are called the **intercepts** of the graph. The **$x$-intercept** is the point **($x$, 0)** where a line crosses (intercepts) the $x$-axis. Similarly, the **$y$-intercept** is the point **(0, $y$)** where a line crosses the $y$-axis.

◆ **TIP:** It is always a good idea to find at least three ordered pairs to make sure they all lie on a line. If they don't all lie on a line, then at least one of the ordered pairs is incorrect. Check your work.

## ⬤ Practice

**Directions:** For Numbers 1 and 2, fill in the table with three ordered pairs that are solutions to the linear equation, then graph the equation.

1. $5x + 4y = 20$

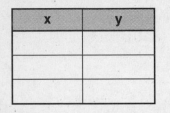

| x | y |
|---|---|
|   |   |
|   |   |
|   |   |

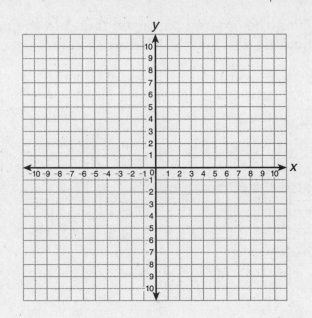

2. $3x + y = 5$

| x | y |
|---|---|
|   |   |
|   |   |
|   |   |

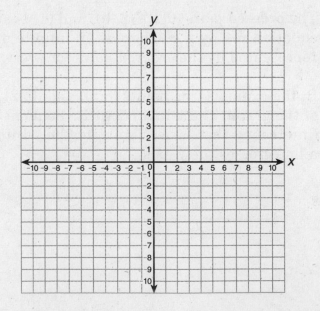

# Representations of Data

When given one representation of data, you can generate different representations of the same data using verbal descriptions, equations, tables, and graphs.

▶ **Example**

The following verbal description, equation, table, and graph all represent the same data.

verbal description: $y$ is equal to $x$ plus two

equation: $y = x + 2$

table:

| x | y |
|---|---|
| −2 | 0 |
| 0 | 2 |
| 2 | 4 |

graph:

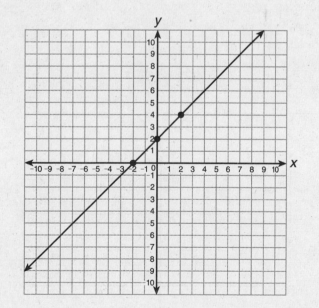

## ◯ Practice

**Directions:** For Numbers 1 through 3, generate three different representations for the one given.

1. *y* is equal to four less than the product of two and *x*.

   equation _____

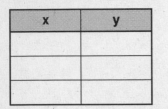

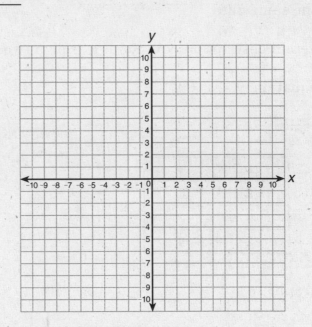

2. $y = -3x$

   verbal description _____

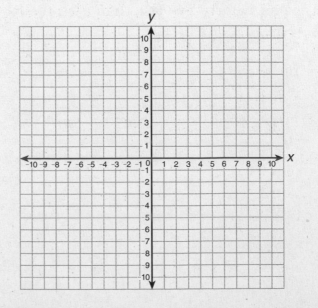

3.

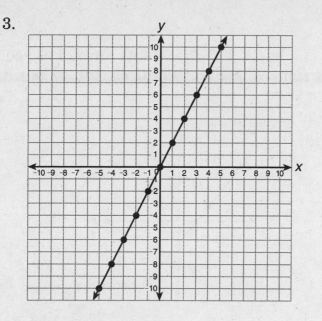

| x | y |
|---|---|
|   |   |
|   |   |
|   |   |

verbal description _____

equation _____

4. How is the following verbal description written as an equation?

   $y$ is equal to forty-five less than the product of ten and $x$.

   A. $y = 45 - 10x$

   B. $y = 10x - 45$

   C. $y = -45 - 10x$

   D. $y = 10(x - 45)$

# Slope

**Slope** is the upward or downward slant of a line. A line that slants upward as you follow it from left to right has a **positive** slope. A line that slants downward as you follow it from left to right has a **negative** slope.

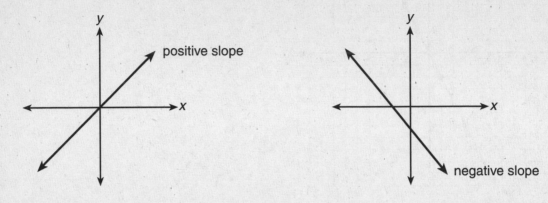

A horizontal line has a **slope of zero**. There is no vertical change in the line as it moves from left to right. A vertical line has an **undefined slope**. There is no horizontal change in the line.

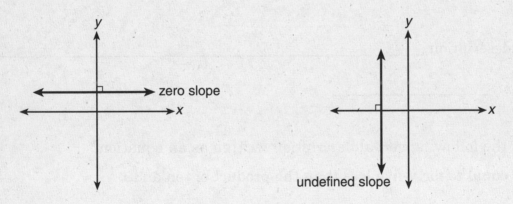

◆ **TIP:** A hori**Z**ontal line has a slope of **Z**ero.

The slope of a line is the ratio of the vertical change of the line to its horizontal change. This ratio is a constant rate of change between any two points on the line. Slope can be determined using the following formula:

$$\text{slope} = \frac{y_2 - y_1}{x_2 - x_1}$$

▷ Example

Find the slope of the line $2x + y = 6$.

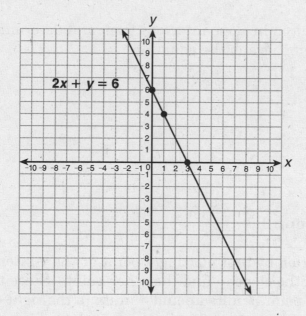

Choose two points on the line to represent $(x_1, y_1)$ and $(x_2, y_2)$.

$(x_1, y_1)$: $(0, 6)$        $(x_2, y_2)$: $(1, 4)$

Substitute the values into the formula to find the slope.

$$\text{slope} = \frac{y_2 - y_1}{x_2 - x_1}$$

$$= \frac{4 - 6}{1 - 0}$$

$$= \frac{-2}{1}$$

$$= -2$$

The slope of the line $2x + y = 6$ is $-2$.

## Slope-intercept form

Linear equations can be written in the following **slope-intercept** form:

$$y = mx + b$$

When written in slope-intercept form, $m$ is the slope of the line, $b$ is the
$y$-intercept, and $x$ and $y$ are the variables. You can plot a point at the $y$-intercept
and then use the slope to graph the linear equation.

▷ **Example**

Write the following equation in slope-intercept form and determine the
slope and $y$-intercept. Then, graph the equation.

$$-3x + 4y = 12$$

$$4y = 3x + 12$$

$$y = \frac{3}{4}x + 3$$

**slope:** $\frac{3}{4}$          **$y$-intercept:** 3

You can graph the equation by first plotting a point at the $y$-intercept,
$(0, 3)$. Then you can use the slope to find the other points. Since the slope
is positive, plot another point 3 units up and 4 units to the right of the
point $(0, 3)$. You can also plot a point 3 units down and 4 units to the left
of $(0, 3)$. The following graph represents $-3x + 4y = 12$.

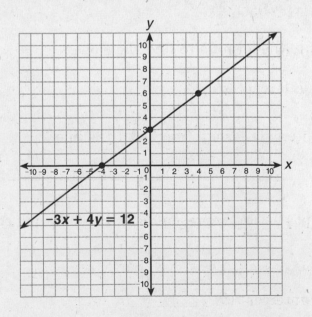

## ◯ Practice

**Directions:** For Numbers 1 through 3, find the slope of the line that passes through the given points.

1. (3, 5) and (0, 7)   slope _____

2. (5, −5) and (1, −3)   slope _____

3. (4, 6) and (−8, −6)   slope _____

**Directions:** Use the following coordinate plane to answer Numbers 4 and 5.

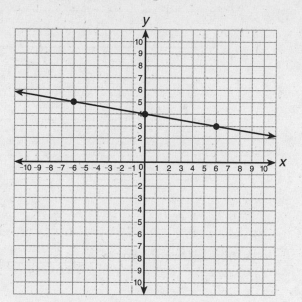

4. Find the slope and *y*-intercept of the line.

   slope (*m*) _____          *y*-intercept (*b*) _____

5. Write an equation in slope-intercept form to represent the line.

   _____

6. Find the slope and *y*-intercept of a line represented by the following equation.

   $-\frac{1}{6}(x + y) = 3$

   slope (*m*) _____          *y*-intercept (*b*) _____

**Directions:** For Numbers 7 and 8, write the given equation in slope-intercept form. Then, find and use the slope and *y*-intercept to graph the given linear equation.

7. $8x + 4y = 16$      slope-intercept form _____

   slope _____

   *y*-intercept _____

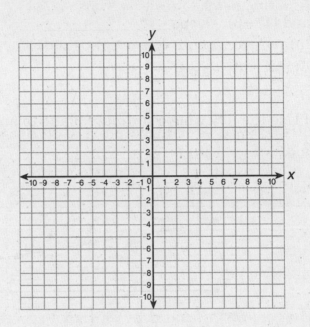

8. $7x - 3y = -12$      slope-intercept form _____

   slope _____

   *y*-intercept _____

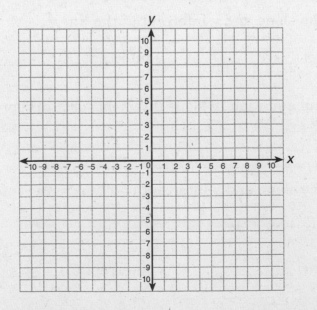

# Graphing Linear Inequalities

You can graph a linear inequality in much the same way that you graph a linear equation. However, the graph of a linear inequality includes a shaded region.

▷ Example

Graph the inequality $x + 4y > 8$.

Step 1: **Replace the inequality symbol with an equal sign.** (This is the equation of the boundary line.)

$x + 4y = 8$

Step 2: **Make a table of ordered pairs that are solutions to the equation of the boundary line.**

| x | y |
|---|---|
| 0 | 2 |
| 4 | 1 |
| 8 | 0 |

Step 3: **Use the ordered pairs to plot and connect the points to form a boundary line.**

If the inequality has a $\geq$ or $\leq$ sign, the boundary line should be solid. This indicates that the points on the line **are** part of the solution. If the inequality has a $>$ or $<$ sign, the boundary line should be dashed. This indicates that the points on the line **are not** part of the solution.

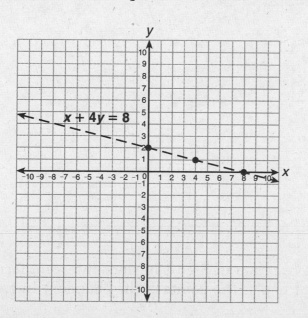

Step 4: **Select a test point not on the line.**

A **test point** is any ordered pair that is not on the boundary line. (0, 0) is always a good choice for a test point if it is not on the boundary line. Substitute the coordinates of the test point for $x$ and $y$ in the inequality.

$$x + 4y > 8$$
$$0 + 4(0) > 8$$
$$0 + 0 > 8$$
$$0 > 6 \quad \textbf{False}$$

Since 0 is not greater than 8, the test point (0, 0) makes the inequality false.

Step 5: **Shade the correct side of the boundary line.**

If the test point makes the inequality **true**, shade the side of the boundary line where the test point is located.

If the test point makes the inequality **false**, shade the side of the boundary line opposite the test point.

In this example, the shading is on the side of the boundary line opposite the test point. Any point in the shaded region is a solution to the inequality.

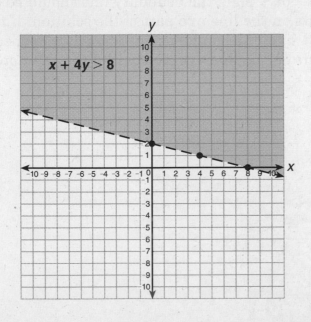

**TIP:** You can also write the equation in Step 1 in slope-intercept form. Then, use the slope and $y$-intercept to plot the points of the boundary line.

## Practice

**Directions:** For Numbers 1 and 2, fill in the table with three ordered pairs that lie on the boundary line of the linear inequality. Then, graph the inequality.

1. $x - y < 2$

| x | y |
|---|---|
|   |   |
|   |   |
|   |   |

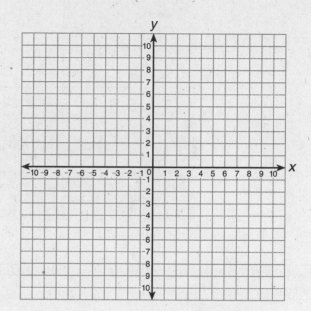

2. $\frac{1}{2}x - y \geq -1$

| x | y |
|---|---|
|   |   |
|   |   |
|   |   |

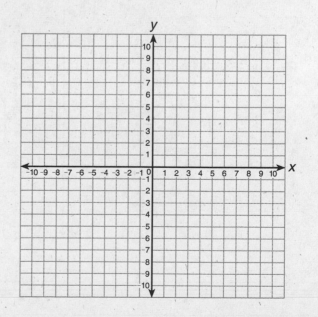

**Directions:** For Numbers 3 and 4, write whether or not the graph represents the given linear inequality. If not, explain why not on the lines below the graph.

3. $5x + 3y \leq 15$

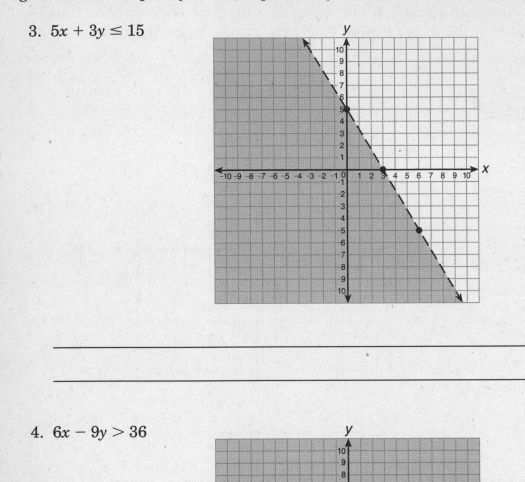

_____

_____

4. $6x - 9y > 36$

_____

_____

# Changes in the Parameters of a Linear Equation

Changing one of the parameters, $m$ or $b$, of a linear equation in slope-intercept form affects the graph of the line.

## Change in $m$

Changing the $m$-value of a linear equation in slope-intercept form changes the slope of the graph of the line. The graph of the new equation will have the same $y$-intercept as the graph of the original equation, but it will have a different slope.

▶ Example

If the $m$-value of the following linear equation is changed to $-\frac{1}{4}$, how will the graph be affected?

$y = 2x + 4$

The following is the new linear equation.

$y = -\frac{1}{4}x + 4$

Graph both the original equation and the new equation on the same coordinate plane.

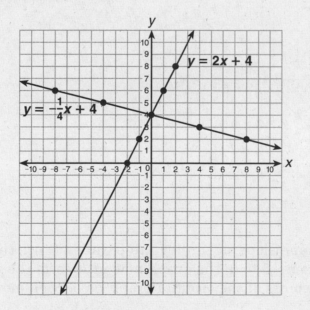

The graphs have the same $y$-intercept, 4. Since the $m$-value has changed from a positive value to a negative value, the graph now falls from left to right instead of rising. Also, the absolute value of $-\frac{1}{4}$ is less than the absolute value of 2, so the line is not as steep.

# Change in *b*

Changing the *b*-value of a linear equation in slope-intercept form changes the *y*-intercept of the graph of the line. The graph of the new equation will have the same slope as the graph of the original equation (the graphs will be parallel), but it will have a different *y*-intercept.

▷ Example

If the *b*-value of the following linear equation is changed to 6, how will the graph be affected?

$$y = x - 5$$

The following is the new linear equation.

$$y = x + 6$$

Graph both the original equation and the new equation on the same coordinate plane.

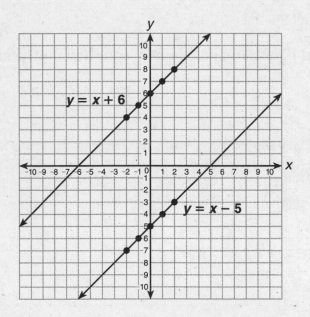

The graphs have the same slope, 1, so they are parallel. Since the *b*-value has changed from −5 to 6, the graph now intersects the *y*-axis at 6 instead of −5. All points of the original graph have been moved up 11 units.

## ◯ Practice

**Directions:** Use the following linear equations to answer Numbers 1 and 2.

$$y = -2x - 3 \quad \text{and} \quad y = 6x - 3$$

1. Graph both linear equations on the following coordinate plane.

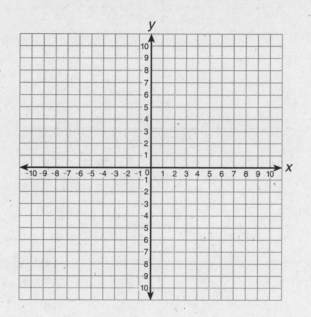

2. What effect does changing the $m$-value have on the graphs of linear equations? Be sure to include the effects of positive versus negative values of $m$.

_____

_____

_____

_____

_____

**Directions:** Use the following linear equations to answer Numbers 3 and 4.

$$y = -x + 2 \quad \text{and} \quad y = -x - 5$$

3. Graph both linear equations on the following coordinate plane.

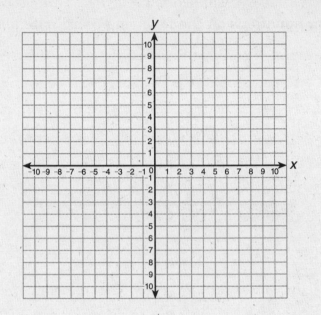

4. What effect does changing the $b$-value have on the graphs of linear equations? Be sure to include the effects of increases versus decreases in the values of $b$.

_____

_____

_____

_____

_____

_____

# Graphing Quadratic Equations

A quadratic equation has the form $y = ax^2 + bx + c$, where $a \neq 0$. The graph of a quadratic equation shows all the solutions to the equation. The graph of a quadratic equation will be a U-shaped curve called a **parabola**. One half of a parabola is a reflection of the other half. The "turn-around" point between these halves is called the **vertex**. The line of reflection, called the **axis of symmetry**, is the vertical line that passes through the vertex. The $x$-coordinate of the vertex is $-\frac{b}{2a}$. Once this value is found, it can be substituted in the equation to find the $y$-coordinate of the vertex. If $a < 0$, then the parabola opens downward, and the $y$-coordinate of the vertex is the **maximum** of the equation. If $a > 0$, then the parabola opens upward, and the $y$-coordinate of the vertex is the **minimum** of the equation. The $y$-intercept of the parabola is $c$.

▷ Example

Make a table of values for and graph the following quadratic equation.

$$y = x^2 - 2x - 8$$

In this equation, $a = 1$, $b = -2$, and $c = -8$. The $x$-coordinate of the vertex is $-\frac{-2}{2(1)} = 1$. Use $x$-values in the table on either side of 1.

| $x$ | $y = x^2 - 2x - 8$ | $y$ |
|---|---|---|
| 4 | $y = 4^2 - 2(4) - 8$ | 0 |
| 3 | $y = 3^2 - 2(3) - 8$ | −5 |
| 2 | $y = 2^2 - 2(2) - 8$ | −8 |
| 1 | $y = 1^2 - 2(1) - 8$ | −9 |
| 0 | $y = 0^2 - 2(0) - 8$ | −8 |
| −1 | $y = (-1)^2 - 2(-1) - 8$ | −5 |
| −2 | $y = (-2)^2 - 2(-2) - 8$ | 0 |

The graph of the quadratic equation is a parabola with a vertex of $(1, -9)$ and an axis of symmetry of $x = 1$. The parabola opens upward and has a minimum value of $-9$. The $y$-intercept is $-8$.

# ⬤ Practice

**Directions:** For Numbers 1 through 4, fill in the table of values for the given quadratic equation (choose *x*-values on either side of the *x*-coordinate of the vertex). Then, graph the equation to show all the solutions.

1. $y = x^2 - 9$

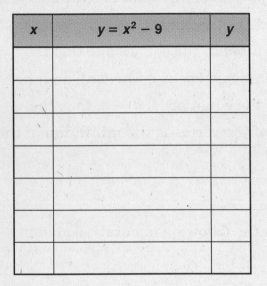
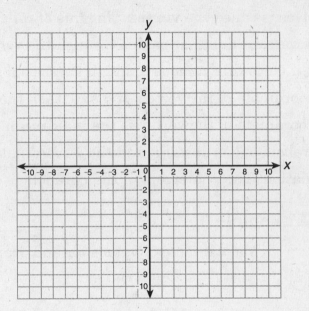

| x | $y = x^2 - 9$ | y |
|---|---|---|
| | | |
| | | |
| | | |
| | | |
| | | |
| | | |

2. $y = -x^2 + 6x + 1$

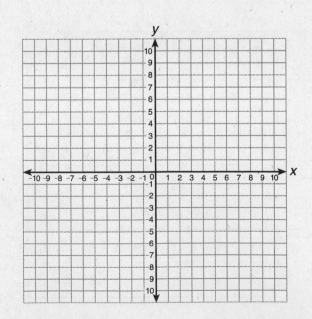

| x | $y = -x^2 + 6x + 1$ | y |
|---|---|---|
| | | |
| | | |
| | | |
| | | |
| | | |
| | | |
| | | |

3. $y = 2x^2 - 10$

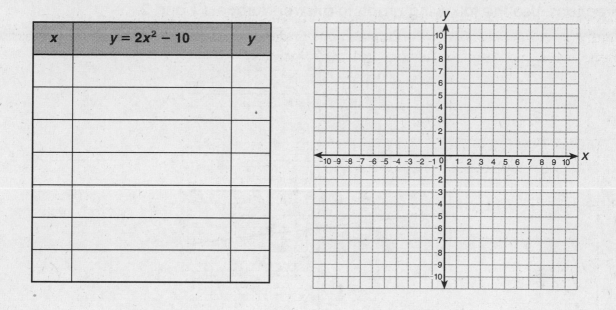

| x | $y = 2x^2 - 10$ | y |
|---|---|---|
| | | |
| | | |
| | | |
| | | |
| | | |
| | | |
| | | |

4. $y = -2x^2 - 4x + 7$

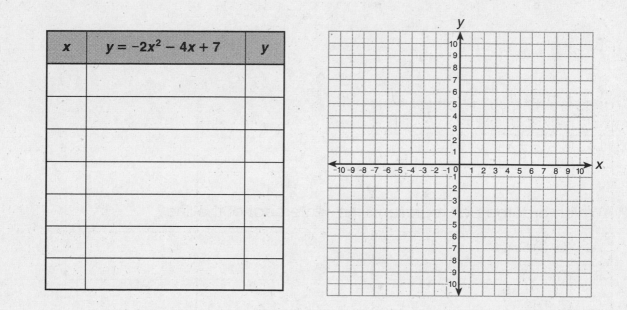

| x | $y = -2x^2 - 4x + 7$ | y |
|---|---|---|
| | | |
| | | |
| | | |
| | | |
| | | |
| | | |
| | | |

# Achievement Practice

**Directions:** Use the following graph to answer Numbers 1 and 2.

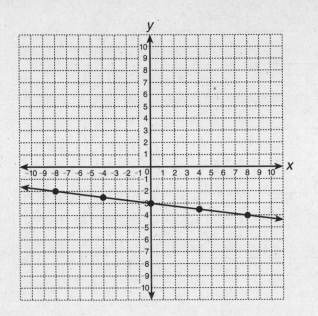

1.  Which linear equation does the graph represent?

    A.  $y = \frac{1}{8}x - 3$

    B.  $y = -\frac{1}{8}x - 3$

    C.  $y = \frac{1}{8}x + 3$

    D.  $y = -\frac{1}{8}x + 3$

2.  Which ordered pair represents the *y*-intercept of the line?

    A.  (0, 3)

    B.  (0, −3)

    C.  (3, 0)

    D.  (−3, 0)

3. Which graph represents $y = 2x^2 - 4x + 5$?

A.

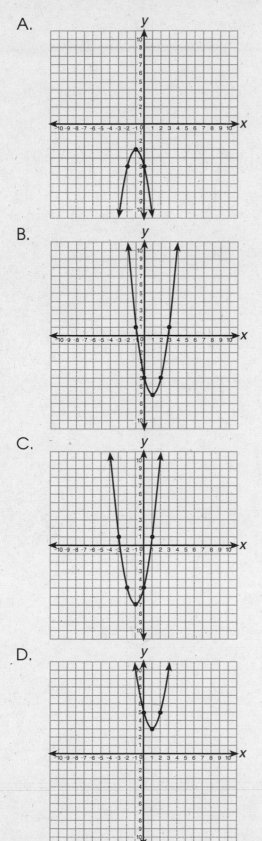

B.

C.

D.

4. Which line has a slope of zero?

A.

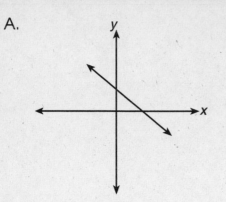

B.

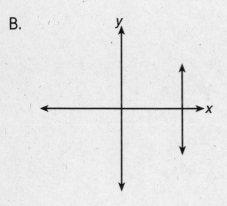

C.

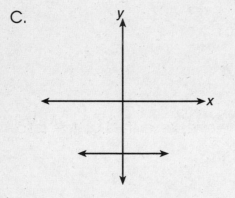

D.

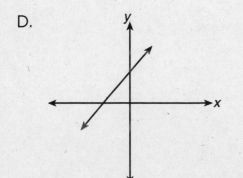

5. Which table of ordered pairs represents the following equation?

$$y = 6x - 7$$

A.

| x | y |
|---|---|
| 3 | 15 |
| 7 | 43 |
| 9 | 57 |

B.

| x | y |
|---|---|
| −1 | −13 |
| 5 | 23 |
| 10 | 53 |

C.

| x | y |
|---|---|
| 0 | 7 |
| 1 | 13 |
| 2 | 21 |

D.

| x | y |
|---|---|
| −2 | 5 |
| 4 | 17 |
| 8 | 55 |

6. What are the slope and *y*-intercept of the line represented by the following equation?

$$5x - y = 10$$

A. $m = 5, b = 10$

B. $m = -5, b = 10$

C. $m = -5, b = -10$

D. $m = 5, b = -10$

7.  Which linear inequality does the following graph represent?

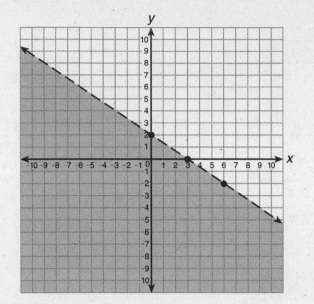

A.  $2x + 3y < 6$

B.  $2x + 3y \leq 6$

C.  $2x + 3y > 6$

D.  $2x + 3y \geq 6$

8.  How is the following verbal description written as an equation?

    $z$ is eight more than double the sum of a number, $n$, and 3.

A.  $z = 8 + 2n + 3$

B.  $z = 8 + 3(n + 3)$

C.  $z = 8 + 2(n + 3)$

D.  $z = 8 + 2(n \div 3)$

9.  Write an equation that represents the numbers in the following table.

| x | y |
|---|---|
| 0 | 2 |
| 6 | 0 |
| 3 | 1 |

_____

10. In the space provided below, write the following equation in slope-intercept form.

$$2x + 5y = 25$$

Graph the equation on the following coordinate plane.

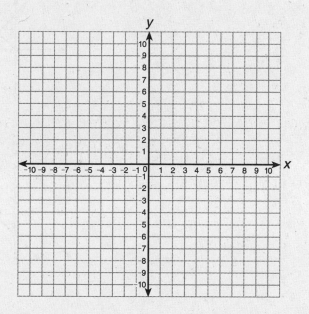

Explain how the graph would be affected if the *m*-value of the equation in slope-intercept form were changed to 3.

_____

_____

_____

# Lesson 6: Systems of Linear Equations

In this lesson, you will solve systems of linear equations by graphing and by using substitution. A **system of linear equations** consists of two or more linear equations. A solution to a system of linear equations is any ordered pair that is a solution to each equation in the system. There are three types of systems of linear equations. Each type has a different number of solutions. A **consistent** system has **exactly one solution**. An **inconsistent** system has **no solution**. A **dependent** system has an **infinite number of solutions**.

## Solving Systems by Graphing

To solve a system of equations by graphing, graph each of the equations in the system. The solution(s), if any, will be the ordered pair(s) of the point(s) of intersection of all the graphs. You can determine the type of system by comparing the slopes and *y*-intercepts of the equations in the system.

**Consistent system**

- exactly one solution
- different slopes

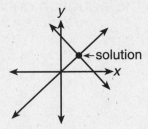

**Inconsistent system**

- no solution
- same slope, different *y*-intercepts

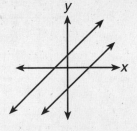

**Dependent system**

- infinite number of solutions
- same slope, same *y*-intercept

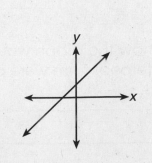

## Consistent systems

A **consistent system** will have exactly one solution. The graphs of the lines in the system will intersect at one point. The solution will be the ordered pair of this point of intersection. In this type of system, the slopes of the graphs in the system are different.

## ▷ Example

Solve the following system of equations graphically.

$$2x - y = 4$$
$$x + 4y = 20$$

Step 1: **Write each equation in the system in slope-intercept form.**

$2x - y = 4$ $\qquad\qquad\qquad\qquad$ $x + 4y = 20$

$-y = -2x + 4$ $\qquad\qquad\qquad\qquad$ $4y = -x + 20$

$y = 2x - 4$ $\qquad\qquad\qquad\qquad$ $y = -\frac{1}{4}x + 5$

**slope:** $2$ $\qquad\qquad\qquad\qquad$ **slope:** $-\frac{1}{4}$

**$y$-intercept:** $-4$ $\qquad\qquad\qquad\qquad$ **$y$-intercept:** $5$

By looking at the slopes, you should be able to determine the type of system that this is and what the graph of this system will show. Since the slopes are different, this system is consistent, and the graph will show a pair of intersecting lines.

Step 2: **Plot each *y*-intercept. Then, find a few other points and draw the graph of each equation on the same coordinate plane.**

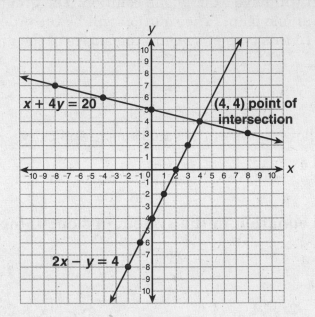

The two lines appear to intersect at (4, 4). This is a possible solution, but you need to check to see that it is a solution to both equations in the system.

Step 3: **Check the point of intersection.**

Substitute the values for the variables in both original equations to see if the ordered pair is a solution to both.

| **Check (4, 4):** $2x - y = 4$ | $x + 4y = 20$ |
|---|---|
| $2(4) - 4 = 4$ | $4 + 4(4) = 20$ |
| $8 - 4 = 4$ | $4 + 16 = 20$ |
| $4 = 4$  **true** | $20 = 20$  **true** |

Since the ordered pair is a solution to both equations in the system, the solution to the system is (4, 4). This is a consistent system of linear equations.

## Inconsistent systems

An inconsistent system will have no solution. The graphs of the lines in the system will be parallel. In this type of system, the slopes of the graphs in the system are the same and the $y$-intercepts of the graphs are different.

▶ **Example**

Solve the following system of equations graphically.

$$x + 4y = 12$$
$$3x + 12y = -24$$

Write each equation in the system in slope-intercept form. Then, graph each of them on the same coordinate plane.

| | |
|---|---|
| $x + 4y = 12$ | $3x + 12y = -24$ |
| $4y = -x + 12$ | $12y = -3x - 24$ |
| $y = -\frac{1}{4}x + 3$ | $y = -\frac{1}{4}x - 2$ |
| **slope:** $-\frac{1}{4}$ | **slope:** $-\frac{1}{4}$ |
| **$y$-intercept:** $3$ | **$y$-intercept:** $-2$ |

The slopes are the same and the $y$-intercepts are different, so the graph will show a pair of parallel lines.

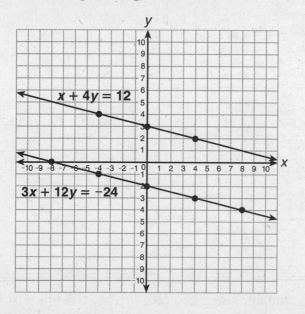

Since parallel lines do not intersect, the system has no solution. This is an inconsistent system of linear equations.

## Dependent systems

A **dependent system** will have an infinite number of solutions. The graphs of the lines in the system will be the same. Since the graphs are the same line, they have an infinite number of points in common. (Any point on the graph of one equation is on the graph of the other equation.) In this type of system, both the slopes and $y$-intercepts of the graphs in the system are the same.

▷ **Example**

Solve the following system of equations graphically.

$$4x - y = -9$$
$$-12x + 3y = 27$$

Write each equation in the system in slope-intercept form. Then, graph each of them on the same coordinate plane.

| | |
|---|---|
| $4x - y = -9$ | $-12x + 3y = 27$ |
| $-y = -4x - 9$ | $3y = 12x + 27$ |
| $y = 4x + 9$ | $y = 4x + 9$ |
| **slope:** 4 | **slope:** 4 |
| **$y$-intercept:** 9 | **$y$-intercept:** 9 |

Both the slopes and $y$-intercepts are the same, so the graph will show one line.

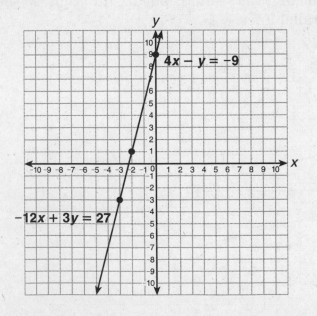

Since the graphs of the equations are the same line, the system has an infinite number of solutions. The solutions are all the ordered pairs that are solutions of either $4x - y = -9$ or $-12x + 3y = 27$. This is a dependent system of linear equations.

## ◯ Practice

**Directions:** For Numbers 1 through 4, solve the system of linear equations graphically. Then, write the type of system for each.

1.  $4x - y = -4$
    $12x - 3y = 24$

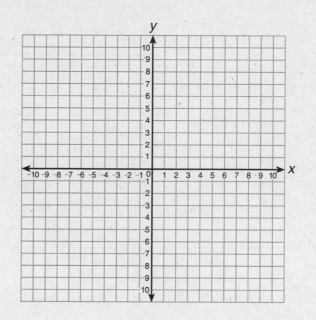

solution(s) _____

The system is _____.

2.  $3x - y = 7$
    $3x - 2y = 8$

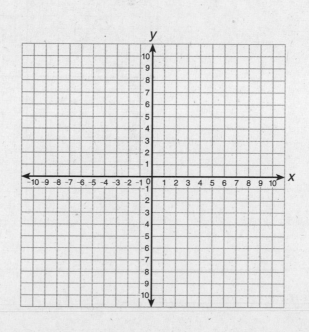

solution(s) _____

The system is _____.

3. $2x + y = 7$
   $-3x + 3y = -6$

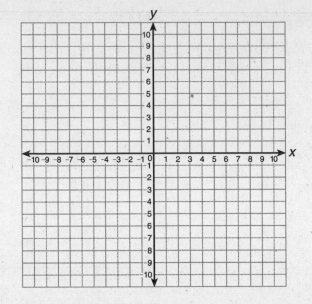

solution(s) _____

The system is _____.

4. $-4x + 6y = -36$
   $2x - 3y = 18$

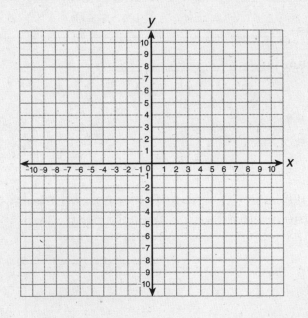

solution(s) _____

The system is _____.

# Solving Systems by Substitution

To solve a system of equations by substitution, solve one of the equations in the system for one of the variables. Then, substitute the equivalent expression for the variable in the other equation.

## ▶ Example

Solve the following system of equations using substitution.

$$4x - 2y = 2$$
$$x - y = -2$$

**Step 1:** **Solve one of the equations in the system for one of the variables.**
Solve the second equation for $y$.

$$x - y = -2$$
$$y = x + 2$$

**Step 2:** **Substitute the expression from Step 1 for the variable in the other equation and solve for the remaining variable.** Substitute
$x + 2$ for $y$ in $4x - 2y = 2$ and solve for $x$.

$$4x - 2y = 2$$
$$4x - 2(x + 2) = 2$$
$$4x - 2x - 4 = 2$$
$$2x = 6$$
$$x = 3$$

**Step 3:** **Substitute the value for the variable in one of the original equations and solve for the other variable.** Substitute 3 for $x$ in the second equation and solve for $y$.

$$x - y = -2$$
$$3 - y = -2$$
$$y = 5$$

Step 4: **Check the values in the original equations.**

| | |
|---|---|
| **Check (3, 5):** $4x - 2y = 2$ | $x - y = -2$ |
| $4(3) - 2(5) = 2$ | $3 - 5 = -2$ |
| $12 - 10 = 2$ | $-2 = -2$ **true** |
| $2 = 2$ **true** | |

Since the ordered pair is a solution to both equations, the solution of the system is (3, 5). This is a consistent system of linear equations.

Sometimes, after you substitute for the first variable and simplify (Step 2), the remaining variable term will drop out. In this case, no variables remain. This will be the case if the system is inconsistent or dependent.

If the equation that is left is **false**, the system is **inconsistent** and has **no solution**. (The graphs will be parallel.)

▷ Example

After Step 2 on the previous page, you may have an equation similar to this one remaining.

$15 = 20$

Since the equation is false, there is no solution. This is an inconsistent system of linear equations.

If the equation that is left is **true**, the system is **dependent** and has an **infinite number of solutions**. The solutions will be all the ordered pairs of all the points on the graph of either equation. (The graphs will be the same.)

▷ Example

After Step 2 on the previous page, you may have an equation similar to this one remaining.

$15 = 15$

Since the equation is true, there are an infinite number of solutions. This is a dependent system of linear equations.

## ⬤ Practice

**Directions:** For Numbers 1 through 4, solve the systems of linear equations using substitution. Then, write the type of system for each.

1. $x - 6y = -12$
   $-2x + 12y = -12$

   solution(s) _____

   The system is _____.

2. $2x - y = -5$
   $3x + y = -10$

   solution(s) _____

   The system is _____.

3. $x + 3y = 5$
   $2x + y = 10$

   solution(s) _____

   The system is _____.

4. $4x + 4y = -8$
   $-3x - 3y = 6$

   solution(s) _____

   The system is _____.

# Achievement Practice

1. Given the following system of linear equations, what will the graphs of the equations in the system look like?

$$3x + 4y = -18$$
$$-12x + 9y = -45$$

   A. same line

   B. intersecting and perpendicular

   C. intersecting and non-perpendicular

   D. parallel

2. What is the solution to the system of linear equations that is graphed on the following coordinate plane?

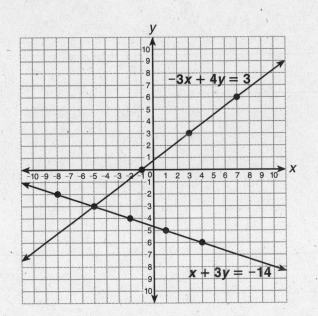

   A. (−5, −3)

   B. (−8, −2)

   C. (3, 3)

   D. (−2, −4)

3.  What is the solution to the following system of linear equations?

$$6x - 3y = -21$$
$$-14x + 7y - 7$$

A.  (0, 7)

B.  (2, 5)

C.  Any solution of either $6x - 3y = -21$ or $-14x + 7y = 7$

D.  There is no solution.

4.  How many solutions does the following system of linear equations have?

$$3x - 5y = 11$$
$$6x - 10y = 22$$

A.  none

B.  one

C.  two

D.  infinite

5.  Use substitution to find the solution to the following system of linear equations.

$$x + 4y = -7$$
$$2x - 3y = 19$$

# Lesson 7: Relationships

In this lesson, you will differentiate and explain types of changes in mathematical relationships.

## Linear and Nonlinear Relationships

You should be able to differentiate between a linear and nonlinear relationship given a table of values, a graph, or an equation of the relationship.

### Tables

Given a table of values, a linear relationship will have a constant rate of change. This constant rate of change represents the slope of the graph of the relationship. A nonlinear relationship will **not** have a constant rate of change.

▷ **Example**

Is the relationship given in the following table linear or nonlinear?

| x | y |
|---|---|
| 3 | 9 |
| 4 | 13 |
| 8 | 29 |
| 11 | 41 |
| 16 | 61 |

Determine the rate of change that occurs between rows of the table. Write the rates as $\left( \dfrac{\text{change in } y}{\text{change in } x} \right)$.

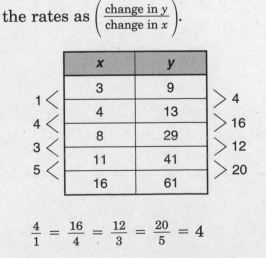

$$\frac{4}{1} = \frac{16}{4} = \frac{12}{3} = \frac{20}{5} = 4$$

Since there is a constant rate of change (4), the relationship is linear.

▷ Example

Is the relationship given in the following table linear or nonlinear?

| x | y |
|---|---|
| 1 | 7 |
| 2 | 13 |
| 6 | 77 |
| 9 | 167 |
| 15 | 455 |

Determine the rate of change that occurs between rows of the table. Write the rates as $\left( \dfrac{\text{change in } y}{\text{change in } x} \right)$.

| x | y |
|---|---|
| 1 | 7 |
| 2 | 13 |
| 6 | 77 |
| 9 | 167 |
| 15 | 455 |

1 ⟨ ... ⟩ 6
4 ⟨ ... ⟩ 64
3 ⟨ ... ⟩ 90
6 ⟨ ... ⟩ 288

$$\frac{6}{1} \neq \frac{64}{4} \neq \frac{90}{3} \neq \frac{288}{6}$$

Since there is not a constant rate of change, the relationship is nonlinear.

# Graphs

The names of the types of relationships tell what the graphs will look like. The graph of a linear relationship will be a line. The graph of a nonlinear relationship will not be a line; rather, it will be some sort of curve.

▷ **Example**

Since the following graph is a curve, the relationship is nonlinear.

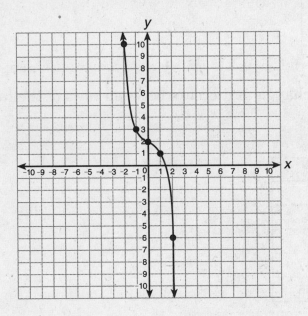

▷ **Example**

Since the following graph is a line, the relationship is linear.

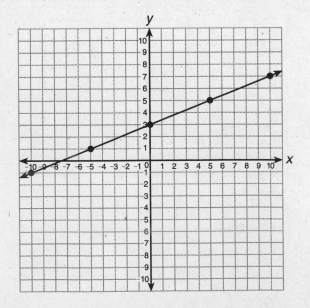

## Equations

The variables in the equation of a linear relationship will both be raised to the first power (as long as they do not occur in a denominator, within a radical sign, or within absolute value symbols). In contrast, at least one variable in the equation of a nonlinear relationship will be raised to some power other than 1.

### ▷ Example

Is the relationship given by the following equation linear or nonlinear?

$$3x + 5y = -8$$

Since both $x$ and $y$ are raised to the first power, the relationship is linear.

### ▷ Example

Is the relationship given by the following equation linear or nonlinear?

$$-7x = 12 - 4y^2$$

Since $y$ is raised to the second power, the relationship is nonlinear.

### ⬤ Practice

**Directions:** For Numbers 1 through 8, identify whether the relationship given by the table, graph, or equation is linear or nonlinear.

1.

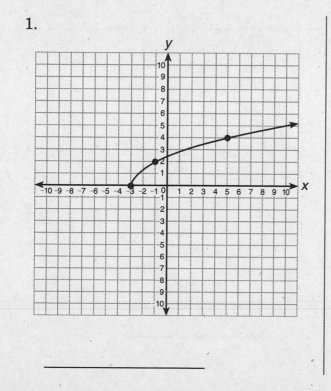

2.

| x | y |
|----|------|
| −2 | −13 |
| 1 | −1 |
| 2 | −13 |
| 7 | −193 |
| 13 | −673 |

_____

3. $5x = 2y - 7$

_____

6. $y = \frac{1}{x} + 3$

_____

4.

| x | y |
|---|---|
| −9 | −58 |
| −7 | −46 |
| −1 | −10 |
| 1 | 2 |
| 5 | 26 |

_____

7.

| x | y |
|---|---|
| −5 | 32 |
| −1 | 12 |
| 0 | 7 |
| 3 | −8 |
| 8 | −33 |

_____

5.

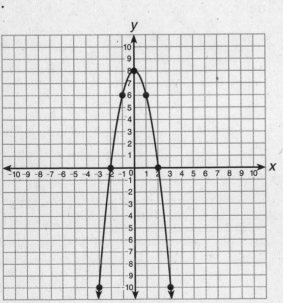

_____

8.

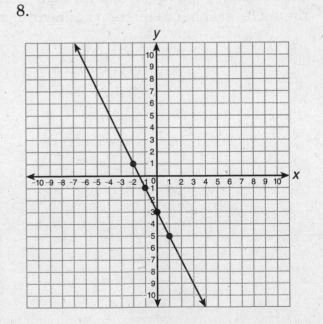

_____

# Continuous and Noncontinuous Relationships

A **continuous** relationship has no breaks or jumps in it. Its graph can be drawn without having to lift the pencil from the paper. If the graph contains any breaks or jumps, then the relationship is **noncontinuous**.

▷ **Example**

The perimeter of a square, $P$, is found by multiplying the side length of the square, $s$, by 4. Is the relationship between the side length and the perimeter of a square continuous or noncontinuous?

The following equation represents the relationship between the perimeter and the side length.

$P = 4s$

The following is the graph of the relationship.

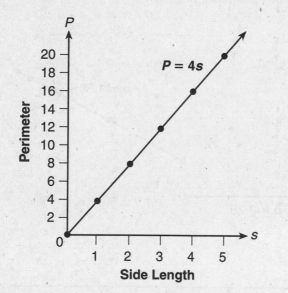

Notice that you can trace over the graph of the relationship without lifting your finger from the graph. Therefore, the relationship between the side length and the perimeter of a square is continuous.

## ▷ Example

A shipping company's price, $p$, is based on the weight, $w$, in pounds of the package it ships. The company's prices are \$1.75 for all packages less than 1 pound, \$3.25 for all packages greater than or equal to 1 pound but less than 3 pounds, and \$1.50 per pound for all packages greater than or equal to 3 pounds. Is the relationship between the weight and the price of a package continuous or noncontinuous?

The following equations represent the relationship between the weight of the packages and the price.

$$p = \begin{cases} 1.75 & \text{for } 0 < w < 1 \\ 3.25 & \text{for } 1 \leq w < 3 \\ 1.50w & \text{for } w \geq 3 \end{cases}$$

The following is the graph of the relationship.

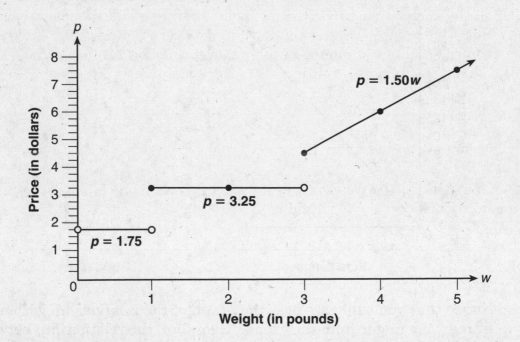

Notice that you cannot trace over the graph of the relationship without taking your finger from the graph. The graph has two breaks and jumps. Therefore, the relationship between the weight and the price of the package is noncontinuous.

## ◯ Practice

1. Freda earns $10 an hour for the first 40 hours that she works in one week. She earns $15 an hour for each hour over 40 that she works in one week. The following equations represent the relationship between the amount that Freda earns in one week, $e$, and the number of hours, $h$, that she works.

$$e = \begin{cases} 10h \text{ for } 0 < h \le 40 \\ 15(h - 40) + 400 \text{ for } h > 40 \end{cases}$$

Is the relationship between the amount that Freda earns in one week and the number of hours that she works continuous or noncontinuous? Explain.

_____

_____

2. Jane opened a savings account with an initial deposit of $150. Since she opened the account, she has neither made any more deposits nor withdrawn any money. She earns interest on her money every day. Is the relationship between the amount of money in the account and the number of days since the account has been opened continuous or noncontinuous? Explain.

_____

_____

What happens to the relationship if Jane deposits money to or withdraws money from the account? Explain.

_____

_____

3. Is the relationship between the length of a blade of grass and time continuous or noncontinuous? Explain.

_____

_____

# Direct and Indirect Variation

**Direct variation** is a relationship between two variables such that when one variable is multiplied by a certain number, the other variable is also multiplied by the same number. The ratio of the values of each variable will be equal. **Indirect variation** is a relationship between two variables such that when one variable is multiplied by a certain number, the other variable is divided by the same number. The ratio of the values of each variable will be reciprocals. Since multiplication and division are inverse operations, indirect variation is sometimes called **inverse variation**.

▷ **Example**

If the rate of speed is held constant, does the time, $t$, an object travels vary directly or indirectly with the distance, $d$, the object travels?

The following equation shows the relationship between time and distance if the rate of speed is held constant at 25 miles per hour.

$$d = 25t$$

Substitute values for one of the variables and solve for the other variable.

Let $t = 6$ and solve for $d$.

$$d = 25t$$
$$= 25 \cdot 6$$
$$= 150$$

Let $t = 3$ and solve for $d$.

$$d = 25t$$
$$= 25 \cdot 3$$
$$= 75$$

Compare the ratio of the values that you substituted with the ratio of the values that you solved for, respectively.

$$\frac{6}{3} = 2 \qquad\qquad \frac{150}{75} = 2$$

Since both of the ratios are the same (2), the time an object travels varies directly with the distance the object travels.

## ▷ Example

If the distance is held constant, does the rate, $r$, of speed of an object vary directly or indirectly with the time, $t$, an object travels?

The following equation shows the relationship between rate and time if the distance is held constant at 100 miles.

$rt = 100$

Substitute values for one of the variables and solve for the other variable.

Let $r = 25$ and solve for $t$.

$$rt = 100$$
$$25 \cdot t = 100$$
$$t = 4$$

Let $r = 5$ and solve for $t$.

$$rt = 100$$
$$5 \cdot t = 100$$
$$t = 20$$

Compare the ratio of the values that you substituted with the ratio of the values that you solved for.

$$\frac{25}{5} = 5 \qquad\qquad \frac{4}{20} = \frac{1}{5}$$

Since the ratios $\left(5 \text{ and } \frac{1}{5}\right)$ are reciprocals, the rate of speed of an object varies indirectly with the time an object travels.

## Graphs

A direct variation is a linear relationship.

▷ **Example**

The following ordered pairs, $(t, d)$, were also found as solutions to the direct variation equation ($d = 25t$) on page 102.

(0, 0), (1, 25), (2, 50), (4, 100), and (5, 125)

The following graph represents the direct variation.

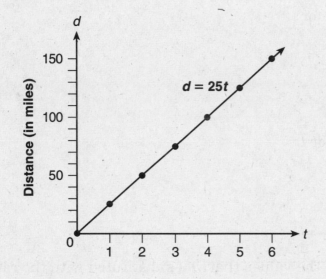

Since the graph is a line, the relationship is linear.

An indirect variation is a nonlinear relationship.

▷ **Example**

The following ordered pairs, $(t, r)$, were also found as solutions to the direct variation equation ($rt = 100$) on page 103.

(1, 100), (2, 50), (5, 20), and (10, 10)

The following graph represents the indirect variation.

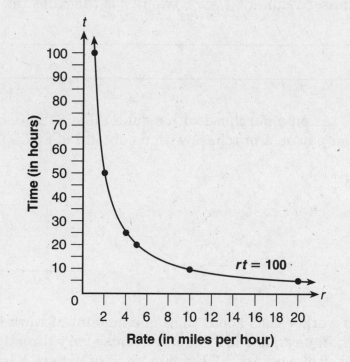

Since the graph is a curve, the relationship is nonlinear.

● **Practice**

1. If the area, $A$, of a rectangle is held constant at 48 cm$^2$, does the length, $l$, of the rectangle vary directly or indirectly with the width, $w$, of the rectangle? Explain. ($A = lw$)

_____

_____

2. If the length of a rectangle is held constant at 8 inches, does the area of the rectangle vary directly or indirectly with the width, $w$, of the rectangle? Explain.

_____

_____

3. Does the amount you pay in sales tax, $t$, vary directly or indirectly with the subtotal, $s$, of your purchase? Explain. ($t = rs$, where $r$ is the sales tax rate)

_____

_____

If you pay \$0.75 in sales tax on a purchase with a subtotal of \$12.50, how much sales tax would you pay on a purchase with a subtotal of \$37.50?

_____

4. If you assume that each worker does about the same amount of work in one day, does the time, $t$, in days, needed to build a house vary directly or indirectly with the number of workers, $n$? Explain. ($b = tn$, where $b$ is the number of worker-days needed to build the house)

_____

_____

If it takes 48 days for 5 workers to build a house, how long would it take 20 workers to build the same house?

_____

# Achievement Practice

1. Which table shows a linear relationship between *x* and *y*?

A.

| x | y |
|---|---|
| −1 | −10 |
| 0 | −8 |
| 3 | −3 |
| 6 | 8 |

B.

| x | y |
|---|---|
| −3 | −17 |
| 2 | −7 |
| 5 | −1 |
| 9 | 7 |

C.

| x | y |
|---|---|
| −6 | −12 |
| 3 | −2 |
| 7 | 8 |
| 10 | 18 |

D.

| x | y |
|---|---|
| −4 | 0 |
| 4 | 9 |
| 8 | 14 |
| 11 | 26 |

2. A mile is 5,280 feet. Does the number of miles vary directly or indirectly with the number of feet? Explain.

_____

_____

_____

_____

3. Which graph shows a noncontinuous relationship?

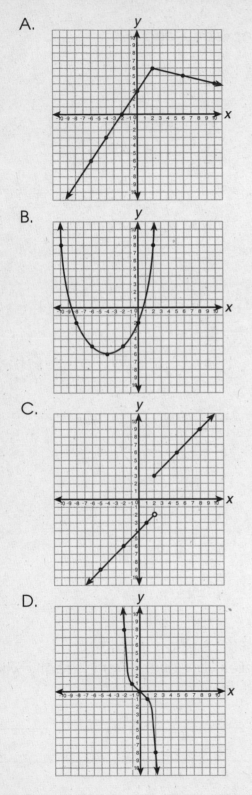

A.

B.

C.

D.

# Lesson 8: Algebraic Concepts

In this lesson, you will review the algebraic concepts of sequences, computation with polynomials, and slope, midpoint, and distance on a coordinate plane.

## Arithmetic Sequences

An **arithmetic sequence** is a number pattern where the **difference** between any two consecutive terms is constant. This difference is called the **common difference ($d$)**. You can use the following formula to find any term in an arithmetic sequence:

$$a_n = a_1 + (n - 1)d$$

where $a_1$ is the first term, $n$ is the position of the term $a_n$, and $d$ is the common difference.

▷ Example

What is the 18th term ($a_{18}$) in the following sequence?

3, 9, 15, 21, 27, . . .

This is an arithmetic sequence with a common difference of 6 (each term is 6 more than the preceding term). Substitute the known values into the formula and simplify.

$$a_n = a_1 + (n - 1)d$$
$$a_{18} = 3 + (18 - 1) \cdot 6$$
$$= 3 + 17 \cdot 6$$
$$= 105$$

The 18th term in the sequence is 105.

What is the $n$th term ($a_n$) in the sequence?

Substitute the known values into the formula and simplify.

$$a_n = a_1 + (n - 1)d$$
$$= 3 + (n - 1) \cdot 6$$
$$= 3 + 6n - 6$$
$$= 6n - 3$$

The $n$th term in the sequence is $6n - 3$.

Practice

**Directions:** For Numbers 1 through 3, write the common difference in each arithmetic sequence.

1. 9, 13, 17, 21, . . . _____

2. 2, 10, 18, 26, 34, . . . _____

3. 16, 7, −2, −11, . . . _____

4. Find the 8th, 11th, and $n$th terms in the following sequence.

    2, 5, 8, 11, 14, . . .

  $a_8$ _____      $a_{11}$ _____      $a_n$ _____

5. Find the 15th, 30th, and $n$th terms in the following sequence.

    200, 195, 190, 185, 180, . . .

  $a_{15}$ _____      $a_{30}$ _____      $a_n$ _____

6. Find the 12th, 18th, and $n$th terms in the following sequence.

    4, 13, 22, 31, 40, . . .

  $a_{12}$ _____      $a_{18}$ _____      $a_n$ _____

7. What is the $n$th term in the following sequence?

    6, 14, 22, 30, 38, . . .

A. $3n + 4$

B. $6n$

C. $8n - 2$

D. $n + 8$

**110**

# Geometric Sequences

A **geometric sequence** is a number pattern where the **ratio** of any two consecutive terms is constant. This ratio is called the **common ratio ($r$)**. You can use the following formula to find any term in a geometric sequence:

$$a_n = a_1 \, r^{(n-1)}$$

where $a_1$ is the first term, $n$ is the position of the term $a_n$, and $r$ is the common ratio.

▷ **Example**

What is the 8th term ($a_8$) in the following sequence?

4, 12, 36, 108, . . .

This is a geometric sequence with a common ratio of 3 (each term is 3 times the preceding term). Substitute the known values into the formula and simplify.

$$a_n = a_1 \, r^{(n-1)}$$
$$a_8 = 4 \cdot 3^{(8-1)}$$
$$= 4 \cdot 3^7$$
$$= 4 \cdot 2{,}187$$
$$= 8{,}748$$

The 8th term in the sequence is 8,748.

▷ **Example**

What is the $n$th term ($a_n$) in the following sequence?

768, 384, 192, 96, . . .

This is a geometric sequence with a common ratio of $\frac{1}{2}$. Substitute the known values into the formula and simplify.

$$a_n = a_1 \, r^{(n-1)}$$
$$= 768 \cdot \left(\frac{1}{2}\right)^{(n-1)}$$

The $n$th term in the sequence is $768 \cdot \left(\frac{1}{2}\right)^{(n-1)}$.

⬤ **Practice**

**Directions:** For Numbers 1 through 3, write the common ratio in each geometric sequence.

1. 1, 4, 16, 64, 256, . . . _____

2. 10, 30, 90, 270, 810, . . . _____

3. 625, 125, 25, 5, 1, . . . _____

4. Find the 7th, 10th, and $n$th terms in the following sequence.

    5, 15, 45, 135, . . .

    $a_7$ _____   $a_{10}$ _____   $a_n$ _____

5. Find the 5th, 7th, and $n$th terms in the following sequence.

    $\frac{2}{3}$, 6, 54, 486, . . .

    $a_5$ _____   $a_7$ _____   $a_n$ _____

6. Find the 6th, 11th, and $n$th terms in the following sequence.

    8,192; 4,096; 2,048; 1,024; . . .

    $a_6$ _____   $a_{11}$ _____   $a_n$ _____

7. What is the $n$th term in the following sequence?

    2,187; −729; 243; −81, . . .

    A. $2{,}187 \cdot \left(-\frac{1}{3}\right)^{(n-1)}$

    B. $2{,}187 \cdot \left(\frac{1}{3}\right)^{(n-1)}$

    C. $2{,}187 \cdot -3^{(n-1)}$

    D. $2{,}187 \cdot \left(-\frac{1}{3}\right)^{(n+1)}$

**112**

# Computation with Polynomials

A **monomial** is an expression that consists of a single term that may be a constant, a variable, or the product of a constant and one or more variables. A **polynomial** is a monomial or the sum of monomials. Each monomial of a polynomial is a **term** of the polynomial. A monomial is a one-term polynomial. A **binomial** is a two-term polynomial. A **trinomial** is a three-term polynomial.

## Adding polynomials

To add polynomials, add the **like terms** by adding the coefficients while leaving the variables and exponents as they are. Like terms are monomials that are constants or have the same variables, each raised to the same power. The following are pairs of like terms.

$5$ and $8$ $\qquad$ $3x$ and $-9x$ $\qquad$ $-y^2$ and $7y^2$ $\qquad$ $6a^2b$ and $-4a^2b$

The following are pairs of **unlike terms**.

$2$ and $x$ $\qquad$ $-5a$ and $7b$ $\qquad$ $-6d^2$ and $9d$ $\qquad$ $-8x^2y$ and $3xy^2$

Algebra tiles can be used to model computations with polynomials. Notice that the shaded tiles represent negative values. Each pair of opposite tiles adds to zero.

The following tiles are 1 unit by 1 unit. They represent 1 and $-1$.

| 1 | | $-1$ |
|---|---|---|

The following tiles are 1 unit by $x$ units. They represent $x$ and $-x$.

| $x$ | | $-x$ |
|---|---|---|

The following tiles are $x$ units by $x$ units. They represent $x^2$ and $-x^2$.

▷ **Example**

Add: $5x + (-2x)$

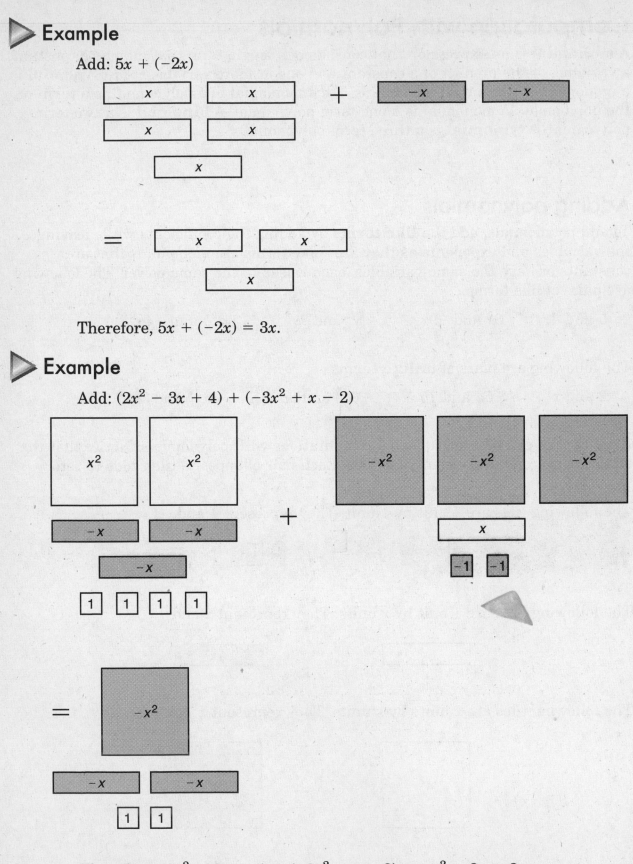

Therefore, $5x + (-2x) = 3x$.

▷ **Example**

Add: $(2x^2 - 3x + 4) + (-3x^2 + x - 2)$

Therefore, $(2x^2 - 3x + 4) + (-3x^2 + x - 2) = -x^2 - 2x + 2$.

## Subtracting polynomials

To subtract polynomials, "add the opposite." Change $-$ to $+$ and every term of the second polynomial to its opposite. Then, follow the rule for addition of polynomials.

### ▶ Example

Subtract: $(-2x^2 + x - 6) - (x^2 + 2x - 5)$

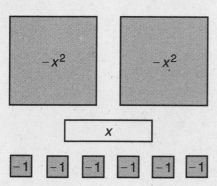 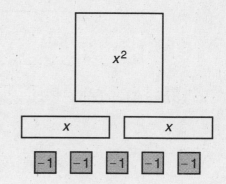

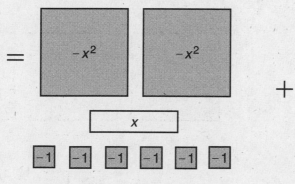 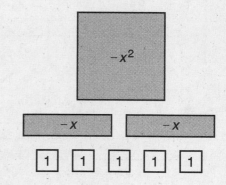

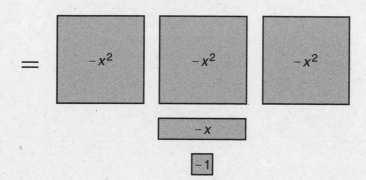

Therefore, $(-2x^2 + x - 6) - (x^2 + 2x - 5) = -3x^2 - x - 1$.

## ⬤ Practice

**Directions:** For Numbers 1 through 6, draw algebra tiles to model each sum or difference. Be sure to shade the tiles that represent negative values. Then, use the model to find the sum or difference.

1. $7x - 4x$

2. $(3x - 4) + (-5x + 1)$

3. $(x^2 - 3x + 4) - (x^2 - 4x - 1)$

4. $-3x^2 - (-2x^2)$

5. $(4x^2 - 5) + (2x + 8)$

6. $(3x^2 + 5x - 2) + (-5x^2 - x + 7)$

## Multiplying a monomial and a polynomial

To multiply a monomial and a polynomial, multiply each term of the polynomial by the monomial (the distributive property). To multiply monomials, multiply the coefficients and add the exponents of like variables. Multiplication of a monomial and a polynomial can be modeled using algebra tiles. The factors will be represented by the sides of a rectangular array, and the product will be represented by the area of the array. (Recall that the area of a rectangle is the product of its length and width.)

▷ **Example**

Multiply: $2x(3x - 5)$

Create a rectangular array that has side lengths of $2x$ and $3x - 5$.

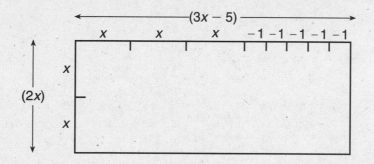

Divide the rectangle into smaller sections by drawing partitions for each value of $\pm x$ and $\pm 1$. Label each of these sections by its area. (Recall the rules for multiplying and dividing positive and negative values.) Then, combine the like terms to find the product.

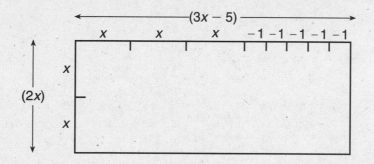

Therefore, $2x(3x - 5) = 6x^2 - 10x$.

## ⬤ Practice

**Directions:** For Numbers 1 through 6, draw algebra tiles to model each product. Then, use the model to find the product. Be sure to shade the tiles that represent negative values.

1. $5(4x + 3)$

2. $x(-2x + 1)$

3. $-3x(x - 4)$

4. $6(5x + 2)$

5. $-2x(6x - 3)$

6. $4x(3x - 7)$

# Slope

Recall from Lesson 5 that slope is the upward or downward slant of a line. The slope of a line is the ratio of the vertical change of the line to its horizontal change. If two points on a line have the coordinates $(x_1, y_1)$ and $(x_2, y_2)$, the slope of the line can be found using the following **slope formula**.

$$\text{slope} = \frac{y_2 - y_1}{x_2 - x_1}$$

▷ Example

What is the slope of $\overleftrightarrow{AB}$ (line $AB$)?

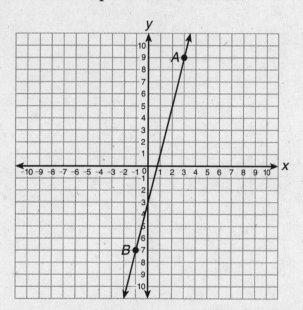

Let $A = (x_1, y_1) = (3, 9)$ and $B = (x_2, y_2) = (-1, -7)$. Substitute these values into the slope formula and simplify.

$$\text{slope} = \frac{y_2 - y_1}{x_2 - x_1}$$

$$= \frac{-7 - 9}{-1 - 3}$$

$$= \frac{-16}{-4}$$

$$= 4$$

The slope of $\overleftrightarrow{AB}$ is 4.

◇ **TIP:** The slope of a segment is the same as the slope of the line that contains the segment.

# Midpoint

The midpoint of a segment is the point that is exactly halfway between the endpoints of the segment. If the endpoints of a segment have the coordinates $(x_1, y_1)$ and $(x_2, y_2)$, the midpoint of the segment can be found using the following **midpoint formula**.

$$M = \left( \frac{x_2 + x_1}{2}, \frac{y_2 + y_1}{2} \right)$$

▷ Example

What is the midpoint of $\overline{AB}$ (segment $AB$)?

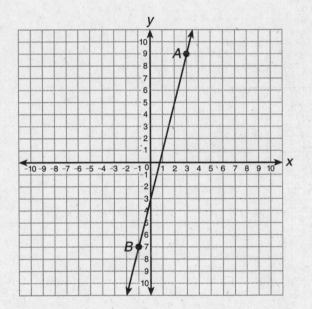

Let $A = (x_1, y_1) = (3, 9)$ and $B = (x_2, y_2) = (-1, -7)$. Substitute these values into the midpoint formula and simplify.

$$M = \left( \frac{x_2 + x_1}{2}, \frac{y_2 + y_1}{2} \right)$$

$$= \left( \frac{-1 + 3}{2}, \frac{-7 + 9}{2} \right)$$

$$= \left( \frac{2}{2}, \frac{2}{2} \right)$$

$$= (1, 1)$$

The midpoint of $\overline{AB}$ is $(1, 1)$.

# Distance Between Points

The distance between two points is the same as the length of a segment that has the points as its endpoints. If two points have the coordinates $(x_1, y_1)$ and $(x_2, y_2)$, the distance between the points, or the length of the segment between the points, can be found using the following **distance formula**.

$$d = \sqrt{(x_2 - x_1)^2 + (y_2 - y_1)^2}$$

## ▷ Example

What is the length of $\overline{AB}$?

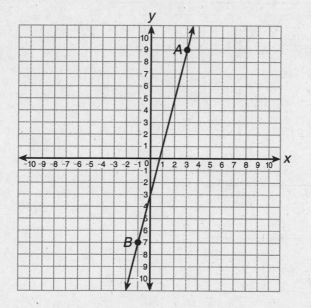

Let $A = (x_1, y_1) = (3, 9)$ and $B = (x_2, y_2) = (-1, -7)$. Substitute these values into the distance formula and simplify.

$$d = \sqrt{(x_2 - x_1)^2 + (y_2 - y_1)^2}$$

$$= \sqrt{(-1 - 3)^2 + (-7 - 9)^2}$$

$$= \sqrt{(-4)^2 + (-16)^2}$$

$$= \sqrt{272}$$

$$= 16.4924225\ldots$$

The length of $\overline{AB}$ is $\sqrt{272}$ or approximately 16.49 units.

▷ **TIP:** If the two points have the same $y$-coordinate, then the distance between them is the absolute value of the difference of their $x$-coordinates. If the two points have the same $x$-coordinate, then the distance between them is the absolute value of the difference of their $y$-coordinates.

## Practice

**Directions:** Use the following coordinate plane to answer Numbers 1 through 8.

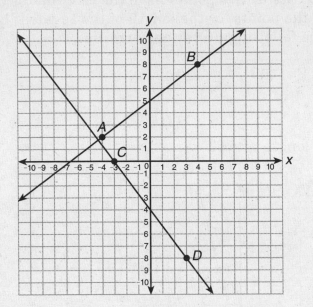

1. What is the slope of $\overleftrightarrow{AB}$? _____

2. What is the slope of $\overleftrightarrow{CD}$? _____

3. What is the midpoint of $\overline{AB}$? _____

4. What is the midpoint of $\overline{CD}$? _____

5. What is the length of $\overline{AB}$? _____

6. What is the length of $\overline{CD}$? _____

7. What is the distance between the midpoints of $\overline{AB}$ and $\overline{CD}$?

   _____

8. Perpendicular lines have slopes that are negative reciprocals (reciprocals that are opposite in sign) of each other. Are $\overleftrightarrow{AB}$ and $\overleftrightarrow{CD}$ perpendicular?

   _____

**Directions:** Use the following information to answer Numbers 9 through 12.

The following map drawn on a coordinate plane shows the locations of some of the summer camp areas and the trails that connect them. Each grid unit on the coordinate plane is equal to 100 feet.

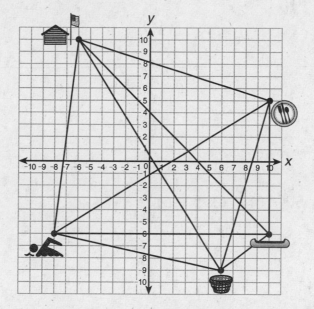

The dining hall is located at (10, 5), the camp office is at (−6, 10), the swim area is at (−8, −6), the craft area is at (6, −9), and the boat docks are at (10, −6).

9. What is the distance between the camp office and the craft area in feet?

_____

10. On the map, what are the slopes of the segments that connect the dining hall to the swim area and the boat docks to the craft area?

_____ and _____

Parallel lines have the same slope. Is the segment that connects the dining hall to the swim area parallel to the segment that connects the boat docks to the craft area?

_____

11. What are the coordinates of the midpoint of the trail that connects the camp office to the swim area?

_____

12. What is the distance between the dining hall and the boat docks in feet?

_____

# Achievement Practice

1. What is the *n*th term in the following sequence?

   94, 113, 132, 141, . . .

   A. $113 - 19n$

   B. $21n + 73$

   C. $19n + 75$

   D. $115 - 21n$

2. Simplify: $(-3y^2 + 5y + 8) - (3y^2 + 6)$

   A. $5y + 14$

   B. $5y + 2$

   C. $-6y^2 + 5y + 2$

   D. $-6y^2 + 5y - 2$

3. Draw algebra tiles to model the following multiplication.

   $2x(3x + 1)$

   $2x(3x + 1) = $ _____

124

4. The locations of two airplanes are shown on the following coordinate plane. What is the slope of the segment from one airplane to the other airplane?

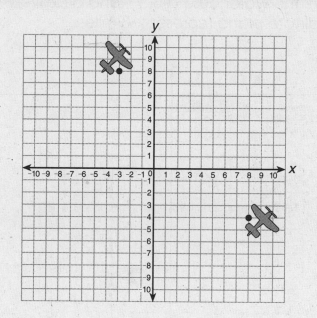

A. $\dfrac{12}{11}$

B. $\dfrac{11}{12}$

C. $-\dfrac{11}{12}$

D. $-\dfrac{12}{11}$

5. What is the 8th term in the following sequence?

$$\dfrac{1}{2}, \dfrac{1}{4}, \dfrac{1}{8}, \dfrac{1}{16}, \cdots$$

A. $\dfrac{1}{32}$

B. $\dfrac{1}{64}$

C. $\dfrac{1}{128}$

D. $\dfrac{1}{256}$

**Directions: Use the following information to answer Numbers 6 and 7.**

The following map drawn on a coordinate plane shows the location of a delivery truck (−8, −9), the warehouse (−3, 7), and a delivery point (2, −5). Each grid unit on the coordinate plane represents 3 miles.

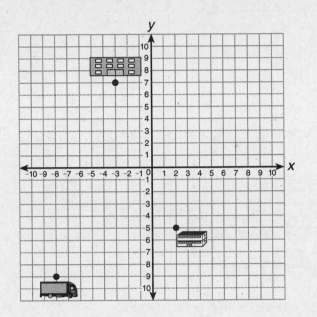

6.  The warehouse expects a call from the truck driver when he is halfway between his present location and the delivery point. What are the coordinates of the point from where the driver will call the warehouse?

    A.  (−7, −3)

    B.  (−3, −7)

    C.  (5, 2)

    D.  (−5, −2)

7.  Even though the truck will drive 51 miles from the delivery point back to the warehouse, what is the distance from the warehouse to the delivery point as the crow flies?

    A.  39 miles

    B.  36 miles

    C.  15 miles

    D.  13 miles

# Unit 3

# Geometry and Spatial Sense

You can thank the ancient Greeks for the word *geometry*—it literally means *earth measurement*. Geometry is everywhere you look. The employees at a publishing company may use a dilation so they can have a small version of their logo on a book cover and a larger version on their T-shirts. An architect who designs a football stadium uses proportion to draw a blueprint that is similar to the actual stadium. Now, think about some of the things around you—buildings, cars, and bridges, for example. They are all built using concepts such as shape, size, and angles. A lot of things wouldn't exist without the application of geometry.

In this unit, you will determine characteristics of angles and solids. You will use proportions to solve problems involving similar figures. You will also use a coordinate plane to represent, analyze, and perform transformations of geometric figures.

## In This Unit

Geometric Concepts
Coordinate Geometry

127

# Lesson 9: Geometric Concepts

In this lesson, you will review the relationships between angles formed from parallel and intersecting lines. You will use proportions to solve problems involving similar figures. You will also review the characteristics and properties of three-dimensional figures.

## Angle Relationships

Two rays that share an endpoint form an **angle**.

The shared point (B) is called the **vertex**.

The rays ($\overrightarrow{BA}$ and $\overrightarrow{BC}$) are called **sides**.

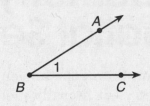

The angle to the right is named $\angle B$, $\angle ABC$, $\angle CBA$, or $\angle 1$. If three letters are used to name an angle, the middle letter names the vertex.

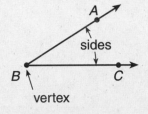

**Complementary angles:** two angles whose measures, denoted by $m$ in front of the angle, have a sum of 90°

$$m\angle WZX + m\angle XZY = 90°$$

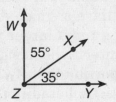

**Supplementary angles:** two angles whose measures have a sum of 180°

$$m\angle ABD + m\angle DBC = 180°$$

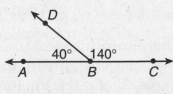

**Vertical angles:** congruent ($\cong$) angles formed by two intersecting lines (congruent angles have the same measure)

$$\angle 1 \cong \angle 3 \qquad \angle 2 \cong \angle 4$$

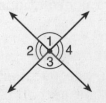

**128**

When two parallel lines are cut by a transversal, certain angle relationships are formed. In the following diagram, parallel lines $m$ and $n$ have been cut by transversal $t$.

Given: $m \parallel n$

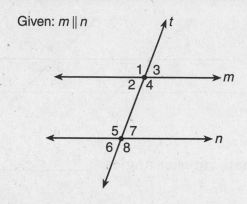

**Interior angles** lie between the two lines that are cut by a transversal.

$\angle 2$, $\angle 4$, $\angle 5$, and $\angle 7$ are interior angles.

**Exterior angles** lie outside the two lines that are cut by a transversal.

$\angle 1$, $\angle 3$, $\angle 6$, and $\angle 8$ are exterior angles.

**Alternate interior angles** are interior angles that lie on opposite sides of a transversal. If the lines are parallel, then the alternate interior angles are congruent.

$\angle 2 \cong \angle 7$     $\angle 4 \cong \angle 5$

**Alternate exterior angles** are exterior angles that lie on opposite sides of a transversal. If the lines are parallel, then the alternate exterior angles are congruent.

$\angle 1 \cong \angle 8$     $\angle 3 \cong \angle 6$

**Corresponding angles** lie on the same side of a transversal, in corresponding positions with respect to the two lines that the transversal intersects. If the lines are parallel, then the corresponding angles are congruent.

$\angle 1 \cong \angle 5$     $\angle 3 \cong \angle 7$     $\angle 2 \cong \angle 6$     $\angle 4 \cong \angle 8$

**TIP:** When parallel lines are cut by a transversal, all of the acute angles are congruent and all of the obtuse angles are congruent. If the transversal is perpendicular to the parallel lines, all of the angles are right angles.

## ⬤ Practice

**Directions:** Use the following diagram to answer Numbers 1 through 10.

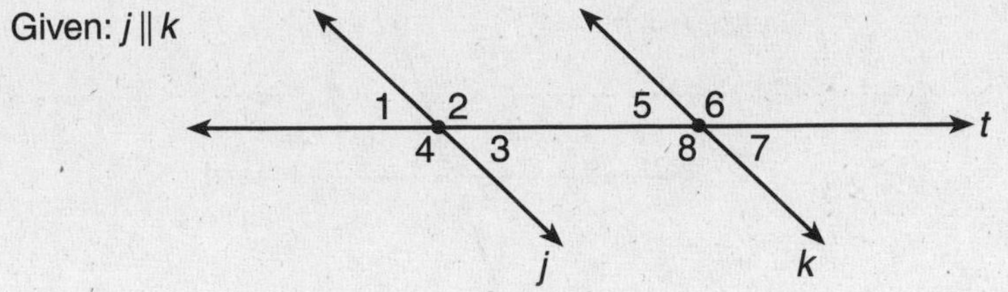

Given: $j \parallel k$

1. List all pairs of alternate interior angles. _____

2. List all pairs of alternate exterior angles. _____

3. List all pairs of corresponding angles. _____

4. List all pairs of vertical angles. _____

5. List two pairs of supplementary angles. _____

6. Name the transversal. _____

7. If $m\angle 2 = 150°$, $m\angle 6 = $ _____.

8. If $m\angle 1 = 30°$, $m\angle 3 = $ _____.

9. Which pair of angles is **not** congruent?

   A. $\angle 2$ and $\angle 4$

   B. $\angle 7$ and $\angle 8$

   C. $\angle 8$ and $\angle 2$

   D. $\angle 8$ and $\angle 6$

10. Which four angles have a sum of 360°?

   A. $\angle 1$, $\angle 2$, $\angle 3$, and $\angle 8$

   B. $\angle 2$, $\angle 4$, $\angle 6$, and $\angle 8$

   C. $\angle 1$, $\angle 3$, $\angle 5$, and $\angle 7$

   D. $\angle 4$, $\angle 6$, $\angle 7$, and $\angle 8$

# Similar Figures

**Similar figures** (~) have the same shape but not necessarily the same size.

Given: $\triangle RST \sim \triangle JKL$

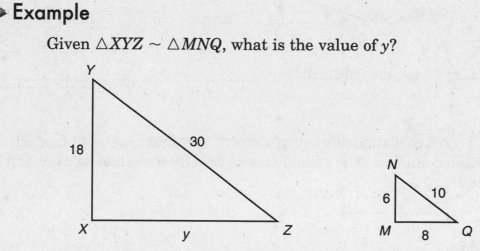

The lengths of the corresponding sides of similar figures are proportional.

$$\frac{RS}{JK} = \frac{RT}{JL} = \frac{ST}{KL}$$

The corresponding angles of similar figures are congruent.

$$\angle R \cong \angle J \qquad \angle S \cong \angle K \qquad \angle T \cong \angle L$$

▶ **Example**

Given $\triangle XYZ \sim \triangle MNQ$, what is the value of $y$?

Set up and solve a proportion using corresponding side lengths.

$$\frac{XZ}{MQ} = \frac{XY}{MN}$$

$$\frac{y}{8} = \frac{18}{6}$$

$$6y = 144$$

$$y = 24$$

The value of $y$ is 24 units.

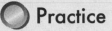

⬤ **Practice**

1. Given *ABCDEF* ~ *GHIJKL*, what is the value of *x*?

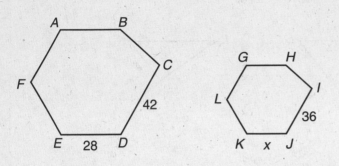

$x = $ _____

2. Given *ABCD* ~ *QRST*, what are the values of *x*, *y*, and *z*?

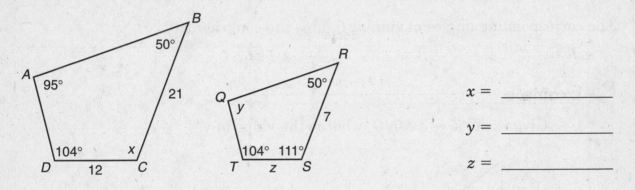

$x = $ _____

$y = $ _____

$z = $ _____

3. Two trees in a park cast shadows one afternoon. The first tree is 48 feet tall and casts a 72-foot shadow. The second tree casts a 30-foot shadow. How tall is the second tree?

    _____

4. Ted is making a model of the Golden Gate Bridge. The bridge's length is 4,200 feet long; the height of its suspension towers is about 750 feet. If Ted makes his model 42 inches long, how tall will he make the suspension towers?

   A.  0.075 inches

   B.  0.75 inches

   C.  7.5 inches

   D. 75 inches

# Solids

A **solid** is a three-dimensional figure that has length, width, and height. Each plane figure of a solid is a **face**. A face that is not a **base** is a **lateral face**. A segment formed when two faces intersect is an **edge**. The point where three or more edges intersect is a **vertex** (or corner). The **net** of a solid is a two-dimensional representation that shows the figure unfolded on a flat surface.

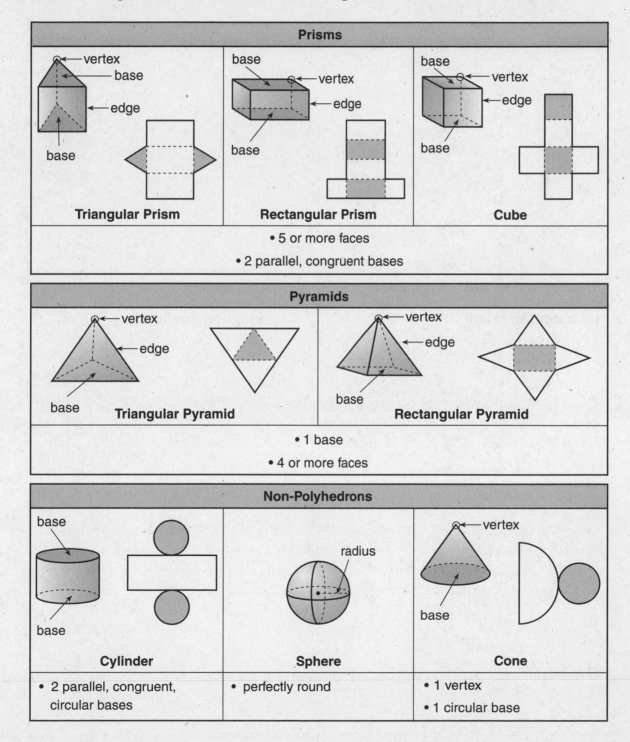

⬤ **Practice**

**Directions:** For Numbers 1 through 4, sketch the net of each given solid.

1. cone

3. cylinder

2. rectangular prism

4. triangular pyramid

# Achievement Practice

**Directions: Use the following triangles to answer Numbers 1 and 2.**

Given: △ABC ~ △DEF

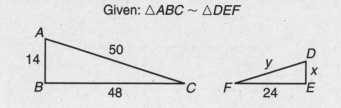

1.  What is the value of *x*?

    A. 6

    B. 7

    C. 8

    D. 9

2.  What is the value of *y*?

    A. 21

    B. 23

    C. 25

    D. 27

3.  What solid does the following net represent?

    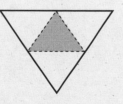

    A. triangular prism

    B. triangular pyramid

    C. cylinder

    D. rectangular pyramid

**Directions: Use the following drawing to answer Numbers 4 through 6.**

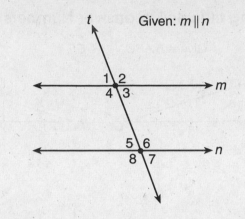

Given: $m \parallel n$

4. What type of angles are $\angle 4$ and $\angle 6$?

    A. vertical

    B. corresponding

    C. alternate interior

    D. alternate exterior

5. Which pair represents alternate exterior angles?

    A. $\angle 2$ and $\angle 8$

    B. $\angle 3$ and $\angle 8$

    C. $\angle 4$ and $\angle 8$

    D. $\angle 5$ and $\angle 8$

6. If $m\angle 5 = 68°$, what are $m\angle 3$ and $m\angle 6$?

    $m\angle 3 = $ _____

    $m\angle 6 = $ _____

# Lesson 10: Coordinate Geometry

In this lesson, you will use the distance and/or slope formula to identify and find missing vertices of figures on the coordinate plane. You will also use the coordinate plane to draw the results of transformations.

## Identifying Triangles and Quadrilaterals

You can use the distance and/or slope formula to identify types of triangles and quadrilaterals. You can also use the formulas to find missing vertices of a quadrilateral.

▷ **Example**

What type of quadrilateral is shown on the following coordinate plane?

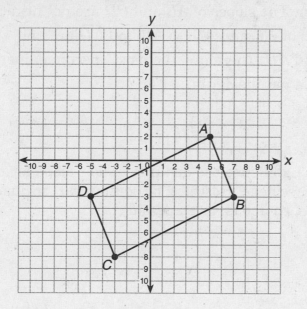

Use the distance formula on page 121 to find the length of each side.

$$AB = \sqrt{(7-5)^2 + (-3-2)^2} = \sqrt{29}$$

$$BC = \sqrt{(-3-7)^2 + [-8-(-3)]^2} = \sqrt{125}$$

$$CD = \sqrt{[-5-(-3)]^2 + [-3-(-8)]^2} = \sqrt{29}$$

$$AD = \sqrt{(-5-5)^2 + (-3-2)^2} = \sqrt{125}$$

Since the opposite sides are congruent, the quadrilateral is a parallelogram. However, can a more specific name be determined? The quadrilateral looks like it could be a rectangle. Remember that a rectangle is a parallelogram with four right angles. Since it has already been shown that the quadrilateral is a parallelogram, you need to determine whether the angles of the quadrilateral measure 90°. The next page shows you how.

Use the slope formula on page 119 to find the slope of each segment.

slope of $\overline{AB} = \frac{-3-2}{7-5} = -\frac{5}{2}$

slope of $\overline{BC} = \frac{-8-(-3)}{-3-7} = \frac{5}{10} = \frac{1}{2}$

slope of $\overline{CD} = \frac{-3-(-8)}{-5-(-3)} = -\frac{5}{2}$

slope of $\overline{AD} = \frac{-3-2}{-5-5} = \frac{5}{10} = \frac{1}{2}$

Two segments will form a right angle if the segments are perpendicular. Two segments are perpendicular if the slopes of the segments are negative reciprocals of each other. The slopes of $\overline{AB}$ and $\overline{CD}$ are not negative reciprocals of the slopes of $\overline{BC}$ and $\overline{AD}$, so $\overline{AB}$ and $\overline{CD}$ are not perpendicular to $\overline{BC}$ and $\overline{AD}$. Therefore, the most specific name for quadrilateral $ABCD$ is a parallelogram.

## ◗ Practice

**Directions:** For Numbers 1 through 3, use the distance and/or slope formula to identify the given triangle (right, scalene, isosceles, or equilateral) or quadrilateral (parallelogram, rectangle, square, rhombus, or trapezoid).

1.

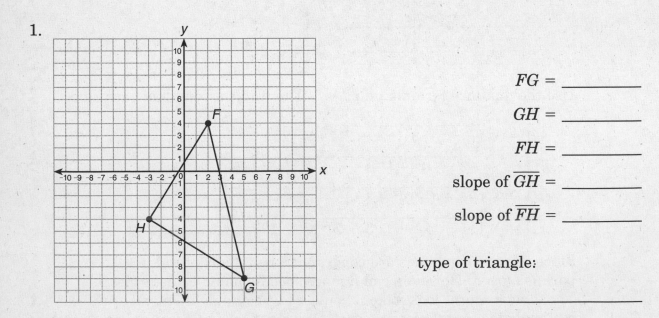

$FG = \underline{\hspace{2cm}}$

$GH = \underline{\hspace{2cm}}$

$FH = \underline{\hspace{2cm}}$

slope of $\overline{GH} = \underline{\hspace{2cm}}$

slope of $\overline{FH} = \underline{\hspace{2cm}}$

type of triangle: 

$\underline{\hspace{4cm}}$

2.

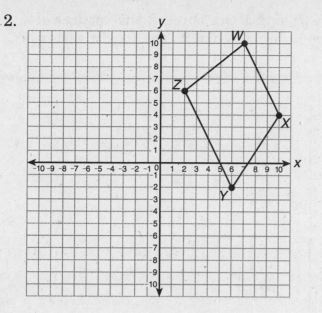

slope of $\overline{WX}$ = _____

slope of $\overline{XY}$ = _____

slope of $\overline{YZ}$ = _____

slope of $\overline{WZ}$ = _____

type of quadrilateral:

_____

3.

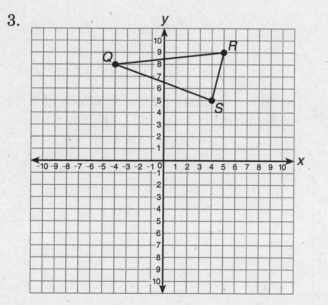

$QR$ = _____

$RS$ = _____

$QS$ = _____

slope of $\overline{RS}$ = _____

slope of $\overline{QS}$ = _____

type of triangle:

_____

4. On the following coordinate plane, *K*, *L*, and *M* are three of the vertices of a square. Use the distance and/or slope formula to plot *N*, the fourth vertex of the square.

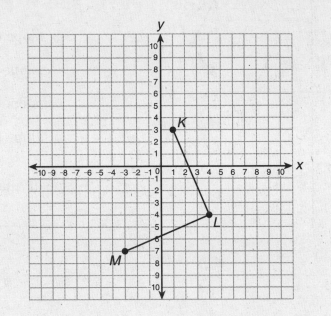

5. On the following coordinate plane, *A*, *B*, and *C* are three of the vertices of a parallelogram. Use the distance and/or slope formula to plot *D*, the fourth vertex of the parallelogram.

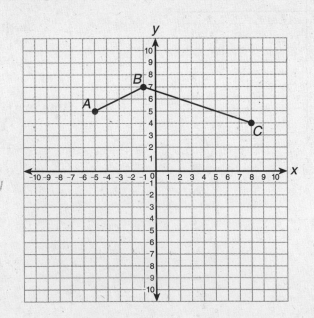

# Transformations

Geometric figures can change position using translations, reflections, rotations, and dilations. You will use a coordinate plane to graph figures that result from these transformations.

## Translation (slide)

A **translation** occurs when you slide a figure without changing anything other than its position. A translated figure has the same size and shape as the original figure.

▷ **Example**

The following coordinate plane shows the translation 5 units up and 2 units to the right of $\triangle CDE$ to form $\triangle C'D'E'$.

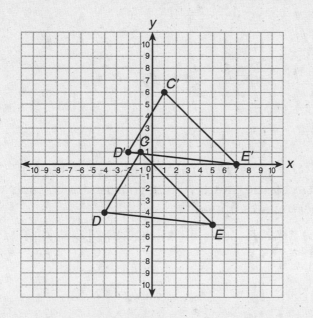

To form $\triangle C'D'E'$, the $x$-coordinate of each vertex of $\triangle CDE$ was increased by 2. The $y$-coordinate of each vertex of $\triangle CDE$ was increased by 5.

| Vertices of $\triangle CDE$ | Vertices of $\triangle C'D'E'$ |
|---|---|
| $C$: $(-1, 1)$ | $C'$: $(1, 6)$ |
| $D$: $(-4, -4)$ | $D'$: $(-2, 1)$ |
| $E$: $(5, -5)$ | $E'$: $(7, 0)$ |

# Reflection (flip)

A **reflection** occurs when you flip a figure over a given line and its mirror image is created. A reflected figure has the same size and shape as the original figure.

▷ **Example**

The following coordinate plane shows the reflection over the *y*-axis of trapezoid *MNOP* to form trapezoid *M'N'O'P'*.

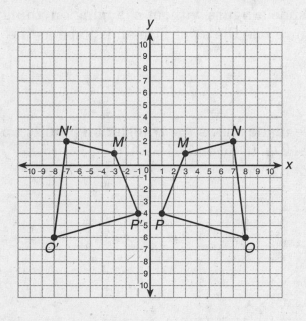

To form trapezoid *M'N'O'P'*, the *y*-coordinate of each vertex of quadrilateral *MNOP* stayed the same. The *x*-coordinate of each vertex of quadrilateral *MNOP* became its opposite.

| Vertices of trapezoid *MNOP* | Vertices of trapezoid *M'N'O'P'* |
|---|---|
| *M*: (3, 1) | *M'*: (−3, 1) |
| *N*: (7, 2) | *N'*: (−7, 2) |
| *O*: (8, −6) | *O'*: (−8, −6) |
| *P*: (1, −4) | *P'*: (−1, −4) |

# Rotation (turn)

A **rotation** occurs when you turn a figure around a given point. Figures can be rotated in a clockwise or counterclockwise direction. A rotated figure has the same size and shape as the original figure.

▷ **Example**

The following coordinate plane shows the 90° clockwise rotation around $J$ of $\triangle JKL$ to form $\triangle JK'L'$.

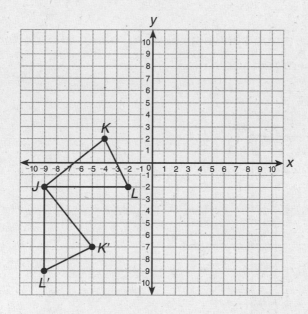

Vertices of $\triangle JKL$

$J$: $(-9, -2)$

$K$: $(-4, 2)$

$L$: $(-2, -2)$

Vertices of $\triangle JK'L'$

$J$: $(-9, -2)$

$K'$: $(-5, -7)$

$L'$: $(-9, -9)$

# Dilation (scale)

A **dilation** occurs when you enlarge or reduce a figure. Figures will be dilated from a point called the **center of dilation**. In this lesson, the center of dilation will be the origin. To perform a dilation on a figure, multiply the coordinates of each vertex by a positive **scale factor**. If the scale factor is less than 1, the dilation will be a **reduction**. If the scale factor is greater than 1, the dilation will be an **enlargement**. In a dilation, the image (the dilated figure) is similar to the original figure.

## ▷ Example

The following coordinate plane shows a dilation, using a scale factor of $\frac{2}{3}$, of rectangle *WXYZ* to form rectangle *W'X'Y'Z'*.

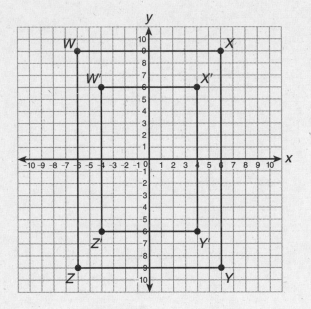

To form rectangle *W'X'Y'Z'*, the *x*- and *y*-coordinates of each vertex of rectangle *WXYZ* have been multiplied by a scale factor of $\frac{2}{3}$. Rectangle *W'X'Y'Z'* is a reduction of rectangle *WXYZ*.

| Vertices of rectangle *WXYZ* | Vertices of rectangle *W'X'Y'Z'* |
|---|---|
| *W*: (−6, 9) | *W'*: (−4, 6) |
| *X*: (6, 9) | *X'*: (4, 6) |
| *Y*: (6, −9) | *Y'*: (4, −6) |
| *Z*: (−6, −9) | *Z'*: (−4, −6) |

## ◉ Practice

**Directions:** For Numbers 1 through 8, draw the given transformation of each figure.

1. reflection over the *y*-axis

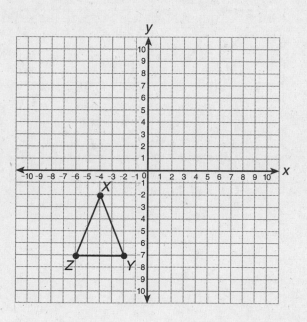

2. 90° counterclockwise rotation around *R*

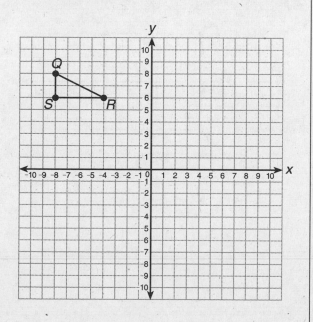

3. translation 8 units left, 7 units down

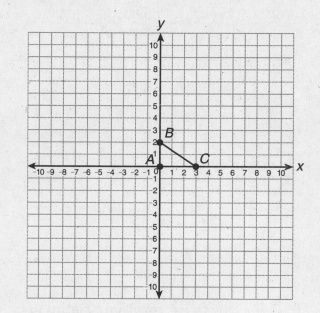

4. translation 8 units up

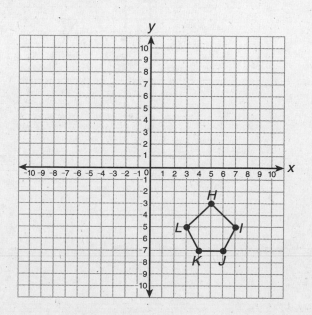

5. dilation using a scale factor of $\frac{1}{2}$

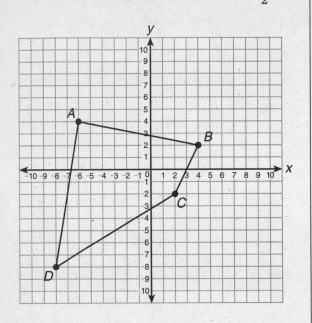

7. reflection over the *x*-axis

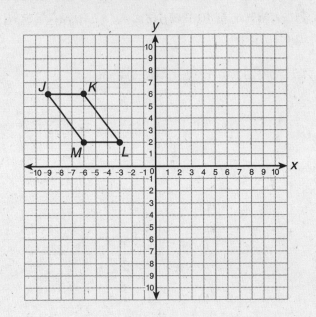

6. 180° clockwise rotation around *M*

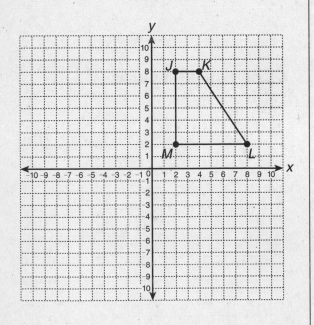

8. dilation using a scale factor of 2

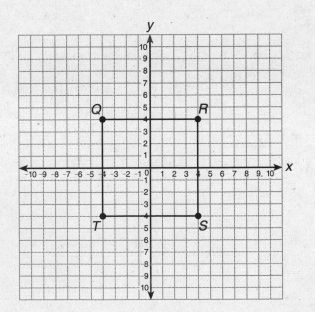

# Achievement Practice

**Directions:** Use the following coordinate plane to answer Numbers 1 and 2.

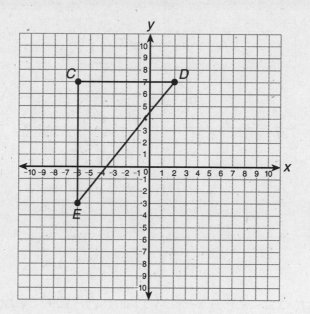

1.  Which of the following **best** describes △*CDE*?

    A.  isosceles

    B.  equilateral

    C.  right

    D.  right and isosceles

2.  If △*CDE* is translated 5 units down and 7 units to the right to form △*C'D'E'*, what will be the coordinates of *E'*?

    A.  (1, −8)

    B.  (−8, 1)

    C.  (−10, −1)

    D.  (0, −9)

**Directions: Use the following coordinate plane to answer Numbers 3 and 4.**

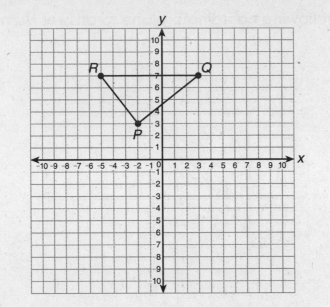

3. If △PQR is reflected over the x-axis to form △P'Q'R', what will be the coordinates of Q'?

   A. (3, −7)

   B. (−3, 7)

   C. (−5, 7)

   D. (−2, −3)

4. If △PQR is translated 10 units down and 2 units to the right to form △P'Q'R', what will be the coordinates of P', Q', and R'?

   P' _____

   Q' _____

   R' _____

**Directions: Use the following coordinate plane to answer Numbers 5 and 6.**

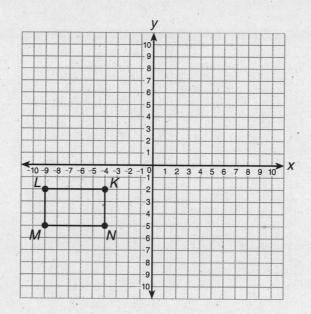

5. If rectangle *KLMN* is rotated 270° clockwise around *K* to form *KL'M'N'*, what will be the coordinates of *M'*?

   A. (3, 1)

   B. (−7, 3)

   C. (−1, −7)

   D. (−4, −10)

6. If *KLMN* is reflected over the *x*-axis to form *K'L'M'N'*, what will be the coordinates of *L'*?

   A. (−9, 2)

   B. (−9, −2)

   C. (9, 2)

   D. (9, −2)

**Directions: Use the following coordinate plane to answer Numbers 7 and 8.**

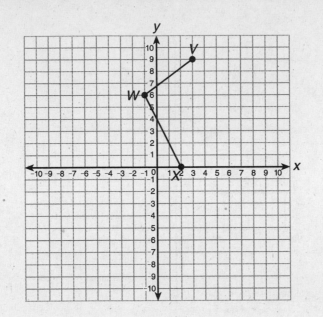

7.  If *V*, *W*, and *X* are three of the vertices of rectangle *VWXY*, what are the coordinates of *Y*?

    A.  (5, 3)

    B.  (6, 3)

    C.  (6, 4)

    D.  (7, 4)

8.  If rectangle *VWXY* is reflected over the *x*-axis, how many of the new vertices will have negative values for both *x*- and *y*-coordinates?

    A.  1

    B.  2

    C.  3

    D.  4

# Measurement

Campbell Hill, the highest point in Ohio, rises 1,549 feet above sea level. Ohio's record low temperature of −39°F was recorded at Milligan, Ohio, in 1899. The area of Ohio is about 116,104 km². Over two thousand years ago, the Greek mathematician Eratosthenes calculated the circumference of Earth to be about 25,000 miles. These are just a few examples of measurement. When you stand on a scale to see how much you weigh, you are measuring. Painters need to know the surface area of buildings so they know how much paint to buy. There are many different ways that measurement is used in the real world.

In this unit, you will use ratios to convert measurements between different measurement systems. You will also use measurement units to solve velocity and density problems. Finally, you will find the sum of angle measures of polygons and use formulas to calculate surface area and volume.

**In This Unit**

Measurement Systems

Geometric Measurement

# Lesson 11: Measurement Systems

In this lesson, you will convert measurements between the U.S. customary system and the metric system. You will also use measurements when using formulas for velocity and density.

## Metric and U.S. Customary Systems

In the metric system, there are a few important prefixes to know that will help you understand the differences between units.

| kilo- | hecto- | deka- | deci- | centi- | milli- |
|---|---|---|---|---|---|
| thousands | hundreds | tens | ten**ths** | hundred**ths** | thousand**ths** |

The values of metric units are based on powers of 10. The values of units in the U.S. customary system vary. In both systems, you can convert from one unit to another using equivalences.

## Length

The following tables show the units of length in order from smallest to largest. They also show the conversion relationships between units of the same system.

| Metric | Conversion |
|---|---|
| **millimeter (mm)** about the thickness of a penny | $1 \text{ mm} = \frac{1}{10} \text{ cm}$ |
| **centimeter (cm)** about the radius of a nickel | $1 \text{ cm} = 10 \text{ mm}$ |
| **meter (m)** about the height of a kitchen table | $1 \text{ m} = 100 \text{ cm}$ |
| **kilometer (km)** about 6 city blocks | $1 \text{ km} = 1{,}000 \text{ m}$ |

| U.S. Customary | Conversion |
|---|---|
| **inch (in.)** about the diameter of a quarter | $1 \text{ in.} = \frac{1}{12} \text{ ft}$ |
| **foot (ft)** about the length of a spaghetti noodle | $1 \text{ ft} = 12 \text{ in.}$ |
| **yard (yd)** about the length of a baseball bat | $1 \text{ yd} = 3 \text{ ft}$ <br> $1 \text{ yd} = 36 \text{ in.}$ |
| **mile (mi)** about 10 city blocks | $1 \text{ mi} = 1{,}760 \text{ yd}$ <br> $1 \text{ mi} = 5{,}280 \text{ ft}$ |

# Weight

The following tables show the units of weight in order from smallest to largest.
They also show the conversion relationships between units of the same system.

| Metric | Conversion |
| --- | --- |
| **milligram (mg)** about the weight of the wing of a housefly | $1 \text{ mg} = \frac{1}{1,000} \text{ g}$ |
| **gram (g)** about the weight of a paper clip | $1 \text{ g} = 1,000 \text{ mg}$ |
| **kilogram (kg)** about the weight of one volume of an encyclopedia | $1 \text{ kg} = 1,000 \text{ g}$ |

| U.S. Customary | Conversion |
| --- | --- |
| **ounce (oz)** about the weight of a slice of bread | $1 \text{ oz} = \frac{1}{16} \text{ lb}$ |
| **pound (lb)** about the weight of a full can of soda | $1 \text{ lb} = 16 \text{ oz}$ |
| **ton (T)** about the weight of a small car | $1 \text{ T} = 2,000 \text{ lb}$ |

# Capacity

The following tables show the units of capacity in order from smallest to largest.
They also show the conversion relationships between units of the same system.

| Metric | Conversion |
| --- | --- |
| **milliliter (mL)** about what an eyedropper holds | $1 \text{ mL} = \frac{1}{1,000} \text{ L}$ |
| **liter (L)** about what a medium plastic soda bottle holds | $1 \text{ L} = 1,000 \text{ mL}$ |
| **kiloliter (kL)** about what a large wading pool holds | $1 \text{ kL} = 1,000 \text{ L}$ |

| U.S. Customary | Conversion |
| --- | --- |
| **teaspoon (tsp)** | $1 \text{ tsp} = \frac{1}{3} \text{ tbsp}$ |
| **tablespoon (tbsp)** | $1 \text{ tbsp} = 3 \text{ tsp}$ |
| **fluid ounce (fl oz)** | $1 \text{ fl oz} = 2 \text{ tbsp}$ |
| **cup (c)** | $1 \text{ c} = 8 \text{ fl oz}$ |
| **pint (pt)** | $1 \text{ pt} = 2 \text{ c}$ |
| **quart (qt)** | $1 \text{ qt} = 2 \text{ pt}$ <br> $1 \text{ qt} = 4 \text{ c}$ |
| **gallon (gal)** | $1 \text{ gal} = 4 \text{ qt}$ <br> $1 \text{ gal} = 8 \text{ pt}$ <br> $1 \text{ gal} = 16 \text{ c}$ |

# Time

The units of time are the same in the U.S. customary system and the metric system. The following tables show the units of time in order from smallest to largest. They also show the conversion relationships between the units.

| Unit | Conversion |
| --- | --- |
| second (s) | $1 \text{ s} = \frac{1}{60} \text{ min}$ |
| minute (min) | 1 min = 60 s |
| hour (hr) | 1 hr = 60 min |
| day (d) | 1 d = 24 hr |

| Unit | Conversion |
| --- | --- |
| week (wk) | 1 wk = 7 d |
| month (mo) | 1 mo ≈ 4 wk |
| year (yr) | 1 yr = 12 mo<br>1 yr ≈ 52 wk<br>1 yr = 365–366 d |

# Temperature

The unit of temperature in the U.S. customary system is **degrees Fahrenheit** (°F). The unit of temperature in the metric system is **degrees Celsius** (°C). The following table shows some common temperatures.

| | U.S. Customary | Metric |
| --- | --- | --- |
| Water freezes | 32°F | 0°C |
| Room temperature | 72°F | 22.2°C |
| Normal human body temperature | 98.6°F | 37°C |
| Water boils | 212°F | 100°C |

# Conversions between systems

Now you will make unit conversions between different systems of measurement. The following table shows the approximate conversion relationships between units of different measurement systems.

|  | Metric to U.S. Customary | U.S. Customary to Metric |
|---|---|---|
| **Length** | 1 cm ≈ 0.3937 in.<br>1 m ≈ 1.094 yd<br>1 km ≈ 0.6214 mi | 1 in. ≈ 2.540 cm<br>1 yd ≈ 0.9144 m<br>1 mi ≈ 1.609 km |
| **Weight** | 1 g ≈ 0.03529 oz<br>1 kg ≈ 2.205 lb | 1 oz ≈ 28.34 g<br>1 lb ≈ 0.4535 kg |
| **Capacity** | 1 mL ≈ 0.03381 fl oz<br>1 L ≈ 1.057 qt | 1 fl oz ≈ 29.57 mL<br>1 qt ≈ 0.9461 L |

There is no simple conversion relationship between the temperature units. Instead, the following formulas are used.

To convert from degrees Celsius to degrees Fahrenheit, use the following formula.

$$°F = \left(\frac{9}{5} \bullet °C\right) + 32$$

To convert from degrees Fahrenheit to degrees Celsius, use the following formula.

$$°C = \frac{5}{9}(°F - 32)$$

▷ **Example**

How many quarts are in 12 liters?

Write the conversion from liters to quarts as a ratio.

$$1 \text{ L} \approx 1.057 \text{ qt}: \frac{1.057 \text{ qt}}{1 \text{ L}}$$

Multiply the original amount (12 L) by this ratio. When you multiply by this ratio, the liters units will divide out, leaving only the quarts unit.

$$12 \text{ L} \cdot \frac{1.057 \text{ qt}}{1 \text{ L}} \approx 12.684 \text{ qt}$$

There are about 12.684 quarts in 12 liters.

▷ **Example**

The normal mean temperature for Columbus in April is 11°C. What is the normal mean temperature for Columbus in April in °F?

Since you are converting from °C to °F, use the following formula.

$$°F = \left( \frac{9}{5} \cdot °C \right) + 32$$

Substitute 11 for °C and simplify.

$$°F = \left( \frac{9}{5} \cdot 11 \right) + 32$$

$$= 19.8 + 32$$

$$= 51.8$$

$$\approx 52$$

The normal mean temperature for Columbus in April is approximately 52°F.

## ◯ Practice

**Directions:** For Numbers 1 through 12, refer to the table of conversions and the formulas for converting temperature on page 155 in order to make the correct conversion. Round your answers to the nearest tenth.

1. 16 cm = _____ in.

2. 90 oz = _____ g

3. 27 km = _____ mi

4. 20 L = _____ qt

5. 59°F = _____ °C

6. 120 mi = _____ km

7. 27 mL = _____ fl oz

8. 42°C = _____ °F

9. 110 m = _____ yd

10. 39 kg = _____ lb

11. 72 in. = _____ cm

12. 11 fl oz = _____ mL

**Directions:** For Numbers 13 through 16, use ratios or formulas to make the conversion. Round your answers to the nearest tenth where necessary.

13. How many meters are in 50 yards? _____

14. Patrick weighs 147 pounds. How many kilograms does Patrick weigh?

_____

15. The melting point of aluminum is 660°C. What is the melting point of aluminum in °F?

_____

16. Gary needs 10 gallons of oil for changing oil in his customers' cars. How many liters of oil does Gary need?

_____

# Using Formulas

Measurement units can be used with formulas for velocity and density.

▷ **Example**

Kyle's family drove 300 miles in 4 hours and 45 minutes. What was the average velocity of their car? Use the following formula.

$$v = \frac{d}{t}$$    where $v$ = velocity

$d$ = distance

$t$ = time

Substitute the known values into the equation and then solve for the unknown variable.

$$v = \frac{d}{t}$$

$$= \frac{300}{4.75}$$

$$= 63.15789473\ldots$$

The average velocity of their car was approximately 63.2 mph.

▷ **Example**

The diamond in Evelyn's necklace has a mass of 1.76 grams and a volume of 0.5 cubic centimeters. What is the density of the diamond? Use the following formula.

$$d = \frac{m}{V}$$    where $d$ = density

$m$ = mass

$V$ = volume

Substitute the known values into the equation and then solve for the unknown variable.

$$d = \frac{m}{V}$$

$$= \frac{1.76}{0.5}$$

$$= 3.52$$

The density of the diamond is approximately 3.52 g/cm$^3$.

## ⬤ Practice

**Directions:** Use the following graph to answer Numbers 1 and 2. Round your answers to the nearest tenth.

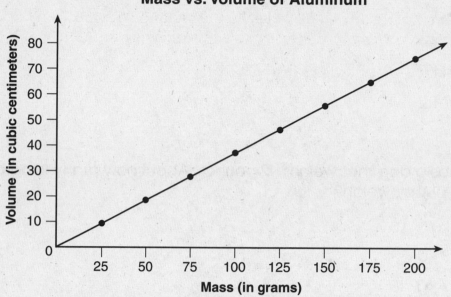

**Mass vs. Volume of Aluminum**

1. What is the density of aluminum? _____

2. What would be the volume of a piece of aluminum that has a mass of 150 grams?

   _____

3. The density of tungsten is 0.697 lb/in.³. If Jeff has 5 in.³ of tungsten, what is the mass of the tungsten?

   _____

4. Casey rode her bicycle 35 miles at an average velocity of 11 miles per hour. How long did it take Casey to ride that distance, in hours and minutes?

   _____

5. Jerome drove 227 miles from Akron to Cincinnati in 4 hours. What was the average velocity of Jerome's trip?

   _____

# Achievement Practice

1. Paula bought 12 gallons of punch for a party. About how many **liters** of punch did Paula buy?

   A. 11.4 L

   B. 12.7 L

   C. 45.4 L

   D. 50.7 L

2. Alice has a dog that weighs 42 pounds. About how many **kilograms** does Alice's puppy weigh?

   A. 19 kg

   B. 52.3 kg

   C. 92.7 kg

   D. 10.9 kg

3. The melting point of cadmium is 610°F. What is the melting point of cadmium in °C?

   A. 339°C

   B. 321°C

   C. 307°C

   D. 301°C

4. On his thirteenth birthday, Andrew measured his height at 65.25 inches tall. About how tall is Andrew in **centimeters**.

   A. 163.1 cm

   B. 160.3 cm

   C. 165.7 cm

   D. 167.1 cm

5. To determine correct postage to mail a letter, Jill has to know how many ounces it weighs. She has a scale that weighs her letter at 119 grams. About how many **ounces** does Jill's letter weigh?

    A. 3.6 oz

    B. 3.8 oz

    C. 4.0 oz

    D. 4.2 oz

6. Graham drove 148 miles from Gallipolis to Springfield. About how many **kilometers** did Graham drive?

    A. 253 km

    B. 238 km

    C. 223 km

    D. 218 km

7. Tracey will earn $6.35 per hour at her part-time job at the coffee shop. How much money will Tracey earn for working 30 hours in one month?

    A. $190.50

    B. $196.50

    C. $212.50

    D. $220.50

8. Jason swam 200 yards in 2 minutes and 45 seconds. What was Jason's velocity in **yards per second**? Round your answer to the nearest tenth.

    $v = $ _____

# Lesson 12: Geometric Measurement

In this lesson, you will find the sum of the interior and exterior angles of a convex polygon. You will also use formulas to find the surface area and volume of solids.

## Angles of a Polygon

You can find the sum of the angle measures of any polygon by measuring with a protractor or just by knowing the number of sides it has.

### Interior angles

An **interior angle of a polygon** is formed by two adjacent sides of a polygon. One way to determine the sum of the measures of the interior angles of a polygon is to divide the polygon into triangles. The sum of the measures of the interior angles of a triangle is 180°. Any polygon can be divided into triangles by drawing diagonals from one vertex to each of the remaining vertices.

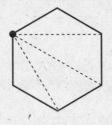

The number of triangles formed is always two less than the number of sides of the polygon. Therefore, the sum of the measures of the interior angles of any polygon can be found using the following formula.

**sum of angles = 180°($n - 2$)**      where $n$ = number of sides of the polygon

▷ Example

Find the sum of the measures of the interior angles of a hexagon.

$$\text{sum of angles} = 180°(n - 2)$$
$$= 180°(6 - 2)$$
$$= 180°(4)$$
$$= 720°$$

The sum of the measures of the interior angles of a hexagon is 720°.

## Exterior angles

An **exterior angle of a polygon** is an angle outside a polygon that forms a linear pair (180° angle) with an interior angle of the polygon. If one side of a polygon is extended, the ray forms an exterior angle with an adjacent side of the polygon. The following diagram shows six exterior angles of a hexagon.

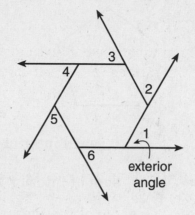

The sum of the measures of the exterior angles of any polygon is 360°.

## ▷ Example

Show that the sum of the exterior angles of a regular hexagon is 360°.

The example on the previous page shows that the measure of each interior angle of a regular hexagon is 120°. Since an interior angle and its adjacent exterior angle are supplementary, the measure of each exterior angle is 60°. Multiply the number of exterior angles (6) by the measure of each angle.

6 • 60 = 360

The sum of the measures of the exterior angles of a regular hexagon is 360°.

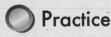 **Practice**

1. Use a protractor to find the measure of each interior angle of the following regular pentagon. Then, find the sum of the interior angle measures of the pentagon.

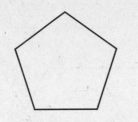

each interior angle measure = _____

sum of interior angle measures = _____

2. Use a protractor to find the measure of each exterior angle of the following equilateral triangle. Then, find the sum of the exterior angle measures of the triangle.

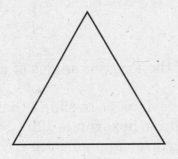

each exterior angle measure = _____

sum of exterior angle measures = _____

3. What is the sum of the exterior angle measures of an octagon? _____

4. What is the sum of the interior angle measures of a decagon (10 sides)?

_____

5. What is the sum of the interior angle measures of a quadrilateral? _____

6. What is the sum of the exterior angle measures of a 15-sided figure? _____

# Surface Area

**Surface area (*S.A.*)** is the measure of the outside of a three-dimensional figure. Since it is an area, the units of surface area are squared units. The following table shows formulas for finding the surface areas of some three-dimensional figures.

| Figure | Formula | |
|---|---|---|
| **prism** | $S.A. = Ph + 2B$ | where $P$ = perimeter of the base<br>$h$ = height<br>$B$ = area of the base |
| **cylinder** | $S.A. = 2\pi rh + 2\pi r^2$ | where $r$ = radius of the base<br>$h$ = height<br>$\pi \approx 3.14$ |
| **pyramid** | $S.A. = \frac{1}{2} P\ell + B$ | where $P$ = perimeter of the base<br>$\ell$ = slant height<br>$B$ = area of the base |

▷ **Example**

What is the surface area of the following cylinder?

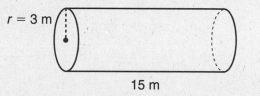

$r = 3\,\text{m}$

$15\,\text{m}$

Substitute the values into the formula.

$$S.A. = 2\pi rh + 2\pi r^2$$

$$= 2 \bullet 3.14 \bullet 3 \bullet 15 + 2 \bullet 3.14 \bullet 3^2$$

$$= 282.6 + 56.52$$

$$= 339.12$$

The surface area of the cylinder is $339.12\,\text{m}^2$.

## ⬤ Practice

1. What is the surface area of the following rectangular prism?

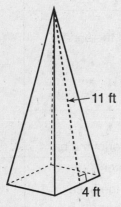

S.A. = _____

2. What is the surface area of the following square pyramid?

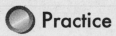

S.A. = _____

3. What is the surface area of the following cube?

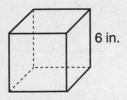

S.A. = _____

4. What is the surface area of the following cylinder? Round your answer to the nearest whole number.

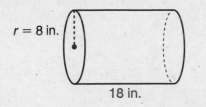

S.A. = _____

5. The following net shows the dimensions of a square pyramid. What is the surface area of the pyramid?

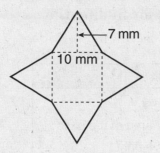

7 mm

10 mm

S.A. = _____

6. What is the slant height of a rectangular pyramid that has a base length of 12 m, a base width of 15 m, and a surface area of 513 m$^2$? Round your answer to the nearest whole number.

$\ell$ = _____

7. What is the surface area of a cylinder that has a radius of 7 yards and a height of 4 yards? Round your answer to the nearest whole number.

S.A. = _____

8. What is the approximate surface area of a cardboard tube that is open at both ends, has a diameter of 3 inches, and has a height of 7.25 inches?

A. 68 ft$^2$

B. 57 ft$^2$

C. 145 ft$^2$

D. 137 ft$^2$

9. What is the surface area of a plastic box that has a length of 7 centimeters, a width of 12 centimeters, and a height of 6 centimeters?

A. 198 cm$^2$

B. 272 cm$^2$

C. 396 cm$^2$

D. 504 cm$^2$

# Volume

**Volume** (*V*) is the amount of space a three-dimensional figure takes up. It is measured in cubic units. The following table shows formulas for finding the volumes of some three-dimensional figures.

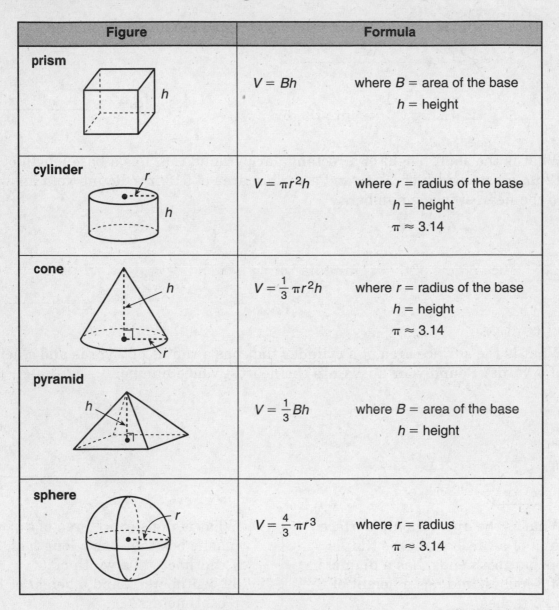

| Figure | Formula |
|---|---|
| prism | $V = Bh$      where $B$ = area of the base<br>$h$ = height |
| cylinder | $V = \pi r^2 h$      where $r$ = radius of the base<br>$h$ = height<br>$\pi \approx 3.14$ |
| cone | $V = \frac{1}{3}\pi r^2 h$      where $r$ = radius of the base<br>$h$ = height<br>$\pi \approx 3.14$ |
| pyramid | $V = \frac{1}{3}Bh$      where $B$ = area of the base<br>$h$ = height |
| sphere | $V = \frac{4}{3}\pi r^3$      where $r$ = radius<br>$\pi \approx 3.14$ |

◆ **TIP:** When calculating the surface area and volume of pyramids, remember that height (*h*) is different from slant height ($\ell$).

## ▷ Example

What is the volume of the following rectangular prism?

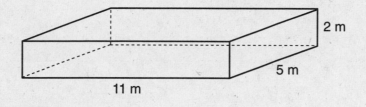

Substitute the values into the formula.

$V = Bh$

$= (11 \bullet 5) \bullet 2$

$= 55 \bullet 2$

$= 110$

The volume of the rectangular prism is 110 m³.

## ◯ Practice

1. What is the volume of the following triangular prism?

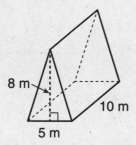

$V = \underline{\hspace{3cm}}$

2. What is the volume of the following rectangular prism?

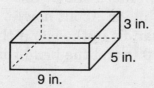

$V = \underline{\hspace{3cm}}$

3. What is the volume of the following cone? Round your answer to the nearest whole number.

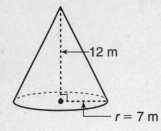

12 m

$r = 7$ m

$V =$ _____

4. What is the volume of the following cylinder? Round your answer to the nearest whole number.

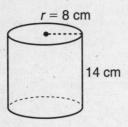

$r = 8$ cm

14 cm

$V =$ _____

5. What is the volume of a square pyramid that has a base length of 4 inches and a height of 5 inches? Round your answer to the nearest whole number.

$V =$ _____

6. What is the radius of a sphere that has a volume of 523.6 cm$^3$?

$r =$ _____

7. About how much ice cream can fit inside a cone that has a diameter of 8 cm and a height of 9 cm?

   A. 75 cm$^3$

   B. 85 cm$^3$

   C. 113 cm$^3$

   D. 151 cm$^3$

8. Farmer McRill has a silo in the shape of a cylinder. About how much grain can fit in the silo if the diameter is 10 ft and the height is 12 ft?

   A. 380 ft$^3$

   B. 942 ft$^3$

   C. 1,570 ft$^3$

   D. 3,800 ft$^3$

**170**

# Achievement Practice

1. What is the volume of this square pyramid?

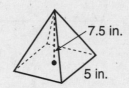

7.5 in.

5 in.

A.   25 in.$^3$

B.   62.5 in.$^3$

C.   93.75 in.$^3$

D.   187.5 in.$^3$

2. What is the sum of the measures of the interior angles of an octagon?

A.   900°

B.   1,080°

C.   1,260°

D.   1,440°

3. Tom's fish tank is 22 inches long, 15 inches tall, and 20 inches wide. How much water would it take to fill the tank to the very top?

A.   6,000 in.$^3$

B.   6,300 in.$^3$

C.   6,600 in.$^3$

D.   6,900 in.$^3$

4. What is the approximate surface area of this cylinder?

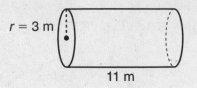

$r = 3\,m$

11 m

    A. 132 m$^2$

    B. 264 m$^2$

    C. 396 m$^2$

    D. 792 m$^2$

5. If the volume of this cone is 307.72 mm$^2$, what is its height?

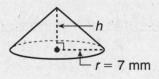

$h$

$r = 7\,mm$

    A. 4 mm

    B. 5 mm

    C. 6 mm

    D. 7 mm

6. What is the approximate volume of a sphere that has a diameter of 7 meters?

    A. 180 m$^3$

    B. 205 m$^3$

    C. 480 m$^3$

    D. 665 m$^3$

7. What is the sum of the measures of the exterior angles of a pentagon?

   A. 720°

   B. 540°

   C. 360°

   D. 180°

8. Karen needs to know the outside surface area (including the bottom) of her tent so she can waterproof it. Her tent has the following dimensions.

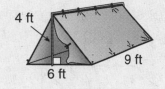

   What is the outside surface area of the tent?

   A. 135 ft$^2$

   B. 144 ft$^2$

   C. 156 ft$^2$

   D. 168 ft$^2$

9. Carmen has a plastic container with a diameter of 8 inches and a height of 10 inches. Which is the best estimate of how much potato salad will fit into the container?

   A. 1,900 in.$^3$

   B. 650 in.$^3$

   C. 500 in.$^3$

   D. 50 in.$^3$

10. What is the surface area and volume of the following pyramid?

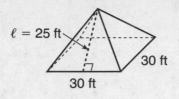

$\ell = 25$ ft

30 ft

30 ft

S.A. = _____

V = _____

11. Tyler built a wooden box for storing items on his parents' deck. The following drawing shows its dimensions.

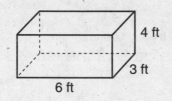

4 ft

3 ft

6 ft

Find the area of each face. Then, find the surface area of the prism by adding the area of all six faces.

S.A. = _____

Use the formula S.A. = Ph + 2B to find the surface area of the prism.

S.A. = _____

How do your calculations for the surface area compare?

_____

_____

# Data Analysis and Probability

Do you look at your favorite baseball team's box score every morning in the newspaper? Perhaps you check the weather forecast to find out what the chance is that it will rain today. Statistics can be used for such things as keeping track of sports teams or recording weather patterns. Probability theory can be used to predict which sports team will win or to determine the chance of precipitation.

In this unit, you will interpret numerical data using the measures of central tendency, range, and percentiles. You will collect, organize, and display data in a variety of graphs. You will also find the probability of compound events and calculate the number of possible outcomes for a situation.

**In This Unit**

Data Analysis

Probability

# Lesson 13: Data Analysis

In this lesson, you will review measures of central tendency as well as range and percentiles. You will identify different types of sampling. You will also construct and interpret different representations of data.

## Measures of Central Tendency

**Measures of central tendency** are used to interpret data by choosing one number to represent all the numbers in a data set. Mean, median, and mode are the measures used for central tendency.

## Mean

The **mean**, sometimes called the "average," is the sum of the numbers in a data set divided by how many numbers are in that set. It is affected by all the numbers in the set. If the data set has **outliers**, the mean may not accurately represent the data. Outliers are values that are noticeably larger or smaller than the rest of the data values.

## Median

The **median** is the middle number in a data set arranged in order of value. If the set contains an even number of numbers, the median is the average of the middle two numbers. The median is usually an accurate representation of data that includes outliers.

## Mode

The **mode** is the number that appears most often in a data set. A data set may contain one mode, more than one mode, or no mode at all. The mode is not affected by outliers.

◆ **TIP:** One way to remember the measures of central tendency is:

**mean:** average        **median:** middle        **mode:** most

# The mean's sensitivity to extremes

Although the mean is usually the most accurate measure of central tendency for describing a data set, it is sometimes better to use the median or the mode.

▷ Example

A total of 101,568 football fans can find a seat in Ohio Stadium to watch the Buckeyes. The following list shows the attendance for six football games. Find the mean attendance for these six games.

99,254

97,353

100,089

101,347

51,871

98,576

$$\text{mean} = \frac{\text{sum of attendance}}{\text{number of games}}$$

$$= \frac{99{,}254 + 97{,}353 + 100{,}089 + 101{,}347 + 51{,}871 + 98{,}576}{6}$$

$$= \frac{548{,}490}{6}$$

$$= 91{,}415$$

The average attendance for the six games is 91,415.

The mean attendance (91,415) is much lower than five of the six numbers. The mean does not really describe the central tendency of this group of numbers. Why? The one extremely low attendance (51,871) has distorted the mean downward.

Because the mean is dependent upon the exact value of each number in the group, it is sensitive to extremely high or extremely low numbers (outliers). If you have such a number in a group for which you want to find the central tendency, you may decide to use the median or the mode instead of the mean. In this example, the median attendance (98,915) is a more accurate measure of central tendency.

# Range

**Range** is a measure of the **variability** in a data set (how the numbers vary or change). To find the range of a data set, calculate the difference between the largest and the smallest numbers.

 Example

What is the range of the following numbers?

9, 18, 20, 24, 19, 48, 8, 15

Subtract the smallest number (8) from the largest number (48).

48 − 8 = 40

The range of the numbers is 40.

## Quartiles and interquartile range

**Quartile** is a word used in statistics to represent one fourth of the data set. The **lower quartile ($Q_1$)** is the median of the lower half of the data set; the **second quartile ($Q_2$)** is the median of the data set; the **upper quartile ($Q_3$)** is the median of the upper half of the data set. The **interquartile range ($IQR$)** of a data set is the difference between the upper quartile and the lower quartile.

▷ Example

What are the lower quartile, upper quartile, and interquartile range of the following numbers?

21, 33, 45, 52, 47, 35, 39, 60, 63, 58, 70, 49

Arrange the numbers from least to greatest and find the medians of the lower and upper halves. Then, subtract the lower quartile from the upper quartile to find the interquartile range.

21, 33, 35, 39, 45, 47, 49, 52, 58, 60, 63, 70

        ↑        ↑        ↑

       **37**      **48**    **59**

  **median of**  **median**  **median of**
  **lower half**           **upper half**

The lower quartile is 37, the upper quartile is 59, and the interquartile range is 22.

# Percentiles

A **percentile** is a measure that tells what percent of the **total frequency**, or the total number of numbers in the data set, is scored at or below that measure. The $p$th percentile of a data set is a value such that at least $p$ percent of the items take on this value or less and at least $(100 - p)$ percent of the items take on this value or more.

To find the $p$th percentile of a data set, arrange the data in order from least to greatest. Compute the **index ($i$)**, the position of the $p$th percentile in the ordered set, by multiplying the percent (written as a decimal) by the total frequency. If the product **is not** an integer, round up. The $p$th percentile is the value in the $i$th position. If the product **is** an integer, the $p$th percentile is the average of the values in positions $i$ and $i + 1$.

▶ **Example**

The following list represents the scores that 15 students received on the last science quiz.

13, 14, 16, 17, 19, 19, 20, 20, 21, 21, 21, 22, 24, 24, 25

If Wilson's score was at the 93rd percentile, what score did Wilson receive?

Convert 93% to a decimal (0.93) and multiply by the frequency (15).

$0.93 \cdot 15 = 13.95$

Since 13.95 is not an integer, round up to 14. Wilson's score is the 14th score listed. Therefore, Wilson received a score of 24 on the quiz.

▶ **Example**

Using the same set of scores in the example above, what score is the 40th percentile?

Convert 40% to a decimal (0.4) and multiply by the frequency (15).

$0.4 \cdot 15 = 6$

Since 6 is an integer, the 40th percentile is the average of the 6th and 7th scores. These scores are 19 and 20. The 40th percentile is 19.5.

◆ **TIP:** The 25th percentile is the lower quartile and the 75th percentile is the upper quartile of the data set.

## Practice

**Directions:** Use the following table to answer Numbers 1 through 4.

### Science Quiz Scores

| Student | 1 | 2 | 3 | 4 | 5 |
|---------|----|----|----|----|----|
| Quiz 1 | 87 | 70 | 90 | 87 | 76 |
| Quiz 2 | 78 | 78 | 87 | 97 | 85 |

1. Find the mean, median, mode, and range of the scores for Quiz 1.

   mean _____    median _____    mode _____    range _____

2. Find the mean, median, mode, and range of the scores for Quiz 2.

   mean _____    median _____    mode _____    range _____

3. Which student placed at the 80th percentile on Quiz 2? _____

   What score did that student receive? _____

4. What score is at the 20th percentile on Quiz 1? _____

**Directions:** Use the following information to answer Numbers 5 and 6.

The following list shows the number of points Shea scored in each basketball game for the month of November.

   26, 18, 17, 21, 23, 23, 29, 24, 14, 45

5. Find the mean, median, mode, and range of the data set.

   mean _____    median _____    mode _____    range _____

   What is the interquartile range of the data set? _____

6. Which measure(s) of central tendency would be appropriate to describe this data set? Why?

   _____

   _____

# Sampling

Using statistical methods, you can make predictions for a large group on the basis of data collected from a subgroup. The large group is called the **population**. The subgroup drawn from the large group is called a **sample**.

You will review four different ways of selecting samples: survey response, random sample, representative sample, and convenience sample. A **survey response** is the information collected from people who respond to a survey. A **random sample** is the collection of data from a subgroup in which each member has an equal chance of being selected. A **representative sample** is a subgroup taken from a larger population of interest. This subgroup is similar to the larger sample in terms of factors that might affect the results of a study. These factors could include, but are not limited to, gender, ethnicity, education level, and age. A **convenience sample** is the collection of data from readily available sources. The larger your sample size is, the better your sample will represent the entire population. With a larger sample, your predictions about the entire population will most likely be more valid than with a smaller sample.

## ◯ Practice

**Directions:** Identify whether the situations in Numbers 1 through 4 would provide a survey response or a random, representative, or convenience sample.

1. Determine the favorite candidate for governor by using the results obtained from asking people a series of questions over the telephone.

   _____

2. Determine the favorite choice for the Super Bowl winner by asking a group of customers in a sporting goods store.

   _____

3. Determine how guests rate the services at a motel by asking every tenth person who checks out of the motel.

   _____

4. Determine the brand of shoes preferred by eighth graders in your town by asking every eighth grader in your math class.

   _____

# Organizing Data

There are two different types of data you will organize—discrete and continuous. **Discrete data** are data that can be counted. **Continuous data** are data that can be assigned an infinite number of values between whole numbers; the assigned values are approximated. Tables and graphs are different ways of organizing data.

## Bar graphs

A **bar graph** is used to compare amounts. A bar graph uses vertical or horizontal bars to show data.

▷ **Example**

The Taft Middle School concession stand sold sports drinks during basketball season. The following table shows how many of each color were sold during the entire season.

**Sports Drink Sales**

| Color | Number Sold |
|-------|-------------|
| Blue | 170 |
| Orange | 106 |
| Red | 145 |
| Purple | 98 |

The data from the table are displayed in the following bar graph.

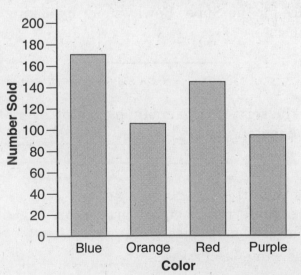

The bar graph gives a better visual representation of the data than the table. The graph lets you compare the different amounts at a glance.

## ◯ Practice

1.  The following table shows the speed of some of the fastest land animals in the world.

### Speed of Land Animals

| Animal | Speed (mph) |
|---|---|
| Cheetah | 70 |
| Pronghorn Antelope | 61 |
| Wildebeest | 50 |
| Lion | 50 |
| Elk | 45 |

Use the information from the table to create a bar graph of the data.

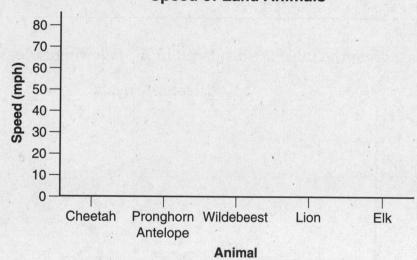

**Directions:** Use the table and the bar graph you created in Number 1 to answer Numbers 2 through 4.

2.  Which animal has the fastest land speed? _____

3.  How much slower is the elk than the pronghorn antelope?

    _____

4.  Which two animals have the same land speed?

    _____

# Histograms

A **histogram** is a type of bar graph that is used to show continuous data. Histograms have the following characteristics:

- The bars are always vertical.
- The bars are always connected to each other.
- The horizontal axis is labeled using intervals.

▷ **Example**

The following table shows the times that the audience took their seats for a movie at the cinema, starting 15 minutes before the start of the movie.

**Theater Arrivals**

| Time | 2:45– 2:46 | 2:47– 2:48 | 2:49– 2:50 | 2:51– 2:52 | 2:53– 2:54 | 2:55– 2:56 | 2:57– 2:58 | 2:59– 3:00 |
|---|---|---|---|---|---|---|---|---|
| Number of People | 8 | 10 | 6 | 18 | 15 | 35 | 40 | 28 |

The data from the table are displayed in the following histogram.

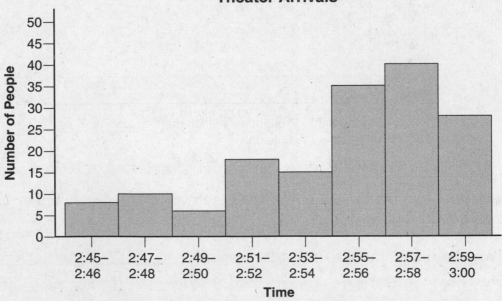

Notice the use of intervals on the horizontal axis. For example, the histogram shows that **between** 2:51 and 2:52, 18 people took their seats for the movie. This is continuous data that requires a histogram.

## ⬤ Practice

1. The following table shows how far from the starting point each participant has reached in the Walk-to-the-Beat Walkathon after 4 hours.

**Walkathon Walkers**

| Miles Walked | 0–2 | 3–4 | 5–6 | 7–8 | 9–10 | 11–12 | 13–14 | 15–16 | 17–18 |
|---|---|---|---|---|---|---|---|---|---|
| Number of People | 0 | 4 | 1 | 5 | 16 | 14 | 2 | 5 | 3 |

Use the information from the table to create a histogram of the data.

**Walkathon Walkers**

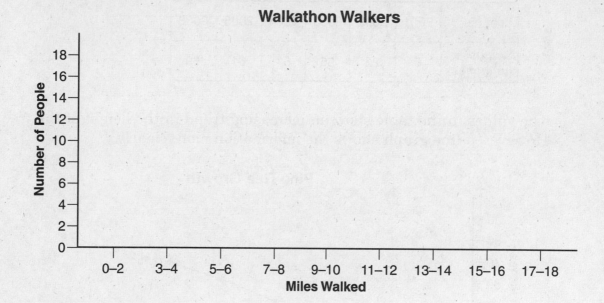

**Directions:** Use the table and the histogram you created in Number 1 to answer Numbers 2 through 4.

2. In what interval is the greatest number of participants? _____

3. How many walkers are farther than 10 miles from the starting point?

   _____

4. In what two intervals can you find the same number of walkers?

   _____

# Line graphs

A **line graph** is useful for showing trends in data over a period of time. A **trend** is a clear direction or pattern in a graph that suggests how the data values will behave in the future. A line graph can have an increasing trend, a decreasing trend, or no trend at all.

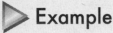 Example

Jill planted a young pine tree in her backyard. She measured it every year to chart its growth. This table shows the tree's height for those years.

**Pine Tree Growth**

| Year | 2001 | 2002 | 2003 | 2004 | 2005 | 2006 |
|---|---|---|---|---|---|---|
| Height (in inches) | 6 | 22 | 36 | 51 | 61 | 69 |

The values in the table show an increasing trend in the height of the tree. However, a line graph shows the information more clearly.

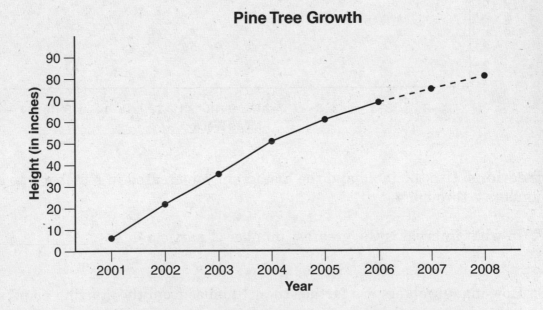

Notice that the trend was continued by extending the line. What inferences can be drawn from the graph? For example, how tall will the tree be in two more years?

The extended line shows that if the trend continues, Jill's tree will reach about 81 inches in 2008.

**186**

## ⬤ Practice

1. Bob took a canoe trip with a group of people. They followed an itinerary, so they knew the number of miles they paddled each day. The following table shows how far along the trip they were by the end of each day.

**Miles in a Canoe**

| Day | 1 | 2 | 3 | 4 | 5 | 6 | 7 | 8 |
|---|---|---|---|---|---|---|---|---|
| Distance From Starting Point (miles) | 12 | 25 | 30 | 37 | 45 | 52 | 60 | 67 |

Use the information from the table to create a line graph of the data.

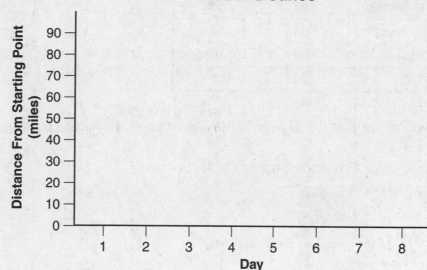

**Directions:** Use the table and the line graph you created in Number 1 to answer Numbers 2 through 4.

2. How many miles did Bob paddle on day 6? _____

3. On which day did Bob travel the greatest number of miles? _____

4. If the overall trend for the distance traveled per day continues, how far would Bob's group have traveled in 10 days?

_____

# Circle graphs

A **circle graph** (sometimes called a **pie chart**) is used to show how different parts of a whole compare to one another. Each part can be expressed as a fraction (the sum of all the parts equals 1) or as a percent (the sum of all the parts equals 100%). A circle graph shows data at one particular time and does not show trends or changes over a period of time.

▷ **Example**

The following table shows the favorite sports of a sampling of eighth graders from the Whitehall School District.

**Favorite Sports**

| Sport | Number of Votes | Percent |
|---|---|---|
| Soccer | 75 | 30% |
| Basketball | 100 | 40% |
| Volleyball | 50 | 20% |
| Tennis | 25 | 10% |
| **Total** | 250 | 100% |

The data from the table are displayed in the following circle graph.

**Favorite Sports**

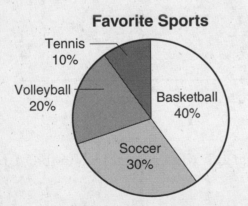

Notice that the circle graph shows percents only. It does not show the actual number of students who favor each sport. You can look at the size of each section of the circle to compare results.

## ⬤ Practice

1. The following table shows how Tara spends her time during a typical day during the school year.

**Tara's Time**

| Activity | Amount of Time (hrs) | Percent |
|----------|:--------------------:|:-------:|
| Sleep | 9 | 38% |
| School | 7 | 30% |
| Sports | 2 | 8% |
| Meals | 1.5 | 6% |
| Homework | 1.5 | 6% |
| Relaxing | 3 | 12% |
| **Total** | 24 | 100% |

Use the information from the table to create a circle graph of the data.

**Tara's Time**

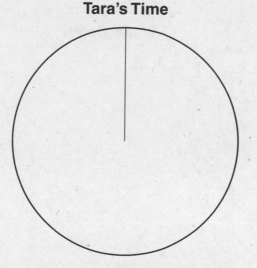

**Directions:** Use the table and the circle graph you created in Number 1 to answer Numbers 2 through 4.

2. What daily activity takes most of Tara's time? _____

3. What two activities together take up as much daily time as relaxing?

_____

4. What two activities together take up as much daily time as sleep?

_____

# Scatterplots

A **scatterplot** is used to show how closely two data sets are related. Plot the values of the variables as ordered pairs and analyze the scatterplot to see how closely the points come to forming a straight line.

 Example

Martha measured how much water was in a deep utility sink, starting when the water was turned on. She checked the depth with a ruler after every minute. The following table shows her results.

**Water Depth**

| Time (min) | 1 | 2 | 3 | 4 | 5 | 6 | 7 | 8 | 9 | 10 | 11 | 12 | 13 | 14 | 15 | 16 |
|---|---|---|---|---|---|---|---|---|---|---|---|---|---|---|---|---|
| Depth of Water (mm) | 20 | 37 | 49 | 64 | 77 | 90 | 105 | 120 | 137 | 150 | 165 | 178 | 193 | 209 | 226 | 240 |

The data from the table is displayed in the following scatterplot.

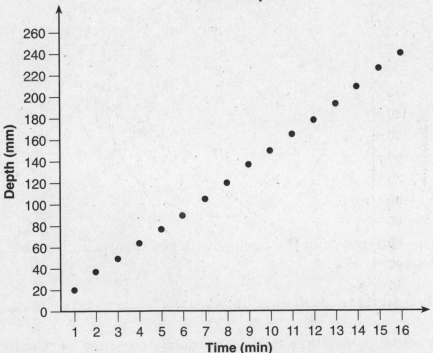

The scatterplot shows that as the number of minutes of running water increases, so does the depth of water in the sink. The points on the scatterplot represent a positive correlation, which will be discussed on the next page.

## Correlation and trend lines

When data are plotted in a scatterplot, the closer the points come to forming a straight, slanted line, the stronger the **correlation**. If you can't see a line formed by the points, then there is probably no correlation. If two data sets are correlated, a **trend line** can be drawn to approximate missing data. A trend line has close to the same number of points above and below it. If a line is vertical or horizontal, correlation is hard to determine because no matter what happens to one variable, the other never changes.

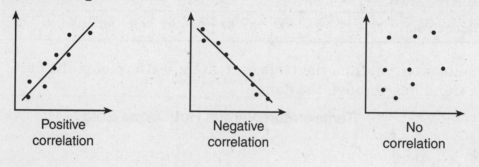

Positive correlation        Negative correlation        No correlation

## ▷ Example

Here is the scatterplot from the previous page with a trend line drawn through the data.

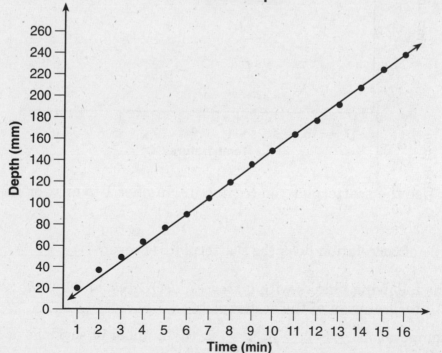

The scatterplot shows a positive correlation between elapsed time and depth of water. The trend line shows this correlation more clearly and allows you to make predictions for possibilities about which you have no specific data. Looking at the trend, you can predict that if Martha lets the water run 2 minutes longer, the water will reach a depth of about 270 mm, provided that the sink does not overflow first.

## ◯ Practice

1. Celia sells hot cocoa at the snack bar near a ski resort. In the following table, she recorded the number of cups of cocoa she served given the temperature that day.

**Temperature Versus Hot Cocoa Sold**

| Temperature (°C) | −10 | −2 | −14 | −15 | −7 | −2 | −14 | −12 | −6 | −8 | −17 | −9 | −4 | −10 |
|---|---|---|---|---|---|---|---|---|---|---|---|---|---|---|
| Hot Cocoa Sold | 78 | 73 | 92 | 100 | 76 | 67 | 94 | 87 | 68 | 85 | 95 | 77 | 79 | 91 |

Use the information from the table to create a scatterplot of the data. Then, draw a trend line through the data.

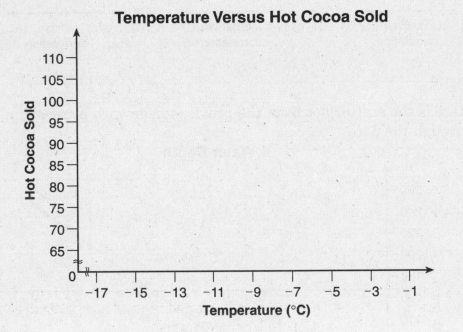

Temperature Versus Hot Cocoa Sold

**Directions:** Use the scatterplot you created in Number 1 to answer Numbers 2 through 4.

2. What type of correlation does the scatterplot represent? _____

3. Fill in the following blanks with *increases*, *decreases*, or *stays the same* to give the best interpretation of the scatterplot.

   As the temperature _____, the number of servings of hot cocoa sold

   _____.

4. Predict the number of servings of hot cocoa Celia will sell if the temperature reaches −19°C.

   _____

**Directions:** Collect data from 12 of your classmates. Find out the number of siblings and number of first cousins each student has. Then, use the data to answer Numbers 5 through 8.

5. Organize the data in the following table.

**Siblings Versus Cousins**

| Number of Siblings | | | | | | | | | | | | |
|---|---|---|---|---|---|---|---|---|---|---|---|---|
| Number of Cousins | | | | | | | | | | | | |

6. Use the information from the table to create a scatterplot of the data.

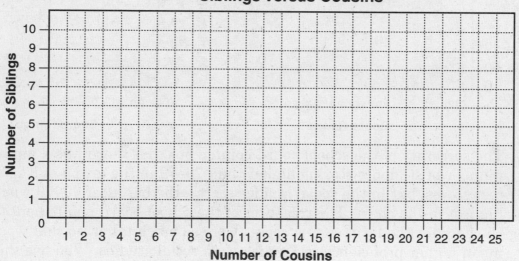

**Siblings Versus Cousins**

7. Do the variables have positive, negative, or no correlation?

_____

8. Interpret the results of your scatterplot.

_____

_____

# Misrepresentations of Data

You have seen that graphs are a good way to organize and interpret data. However, graphs and other visual displays of data can be used to distort data so that it looks as though it is showing something completely different.

▷ **Example**

Every eighth grader in the district took the same tests in English and social studies. The top scores are shown in the following histograms. School board officers were trying to decide if the students in the district were more proficient in English or social studies.

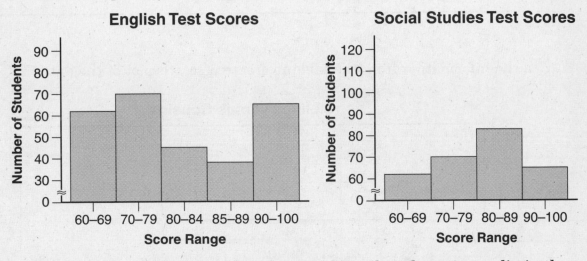

The secretary of the school board pointed out that there was a dip in the number of students scoring higher than 70–79 in the graph of English test scores, but in the social studies scores, the bar after 70–79 was the highest in the chart. The treasurer of the school board pointed out that the bars for the English test scores were so much taller, so that would mean higher proficiency in English than social studies. Who has the better argument?

These graphs are misleading for different reasons. The histogram of English scores does not have equal intervals of score ranges. The third and fourth bars have intervals of 5, while all other bars have intervals of 10.

The vertical scale on the social studies histogram jumps from 0 to 60, whereas the vertical scale on the English histogram jumps from 0 to 30. As a result, the bar for scores 60–69 in the social studies histogram looks a lot smaller than the bar for scores 60–69 in the English histogram even though both bars show the same number of students.

In fact, both graphs have the exact same number of students in each of the intervals of 60–69, 70–79, 80–89, and 90–100. The graphs look very different, which affects interpretation.

## ⬤ Practice

**Directions:** Use the following information to answer Numbers 1 through 3.

The Booster Club sold food items at a stand during a community art fair. The parents in the Booster Club wanted to see how many of each food type sold, so two volunteers each made a bar graph of all food items sold and presented the graphs to the other members of the Booster Club.

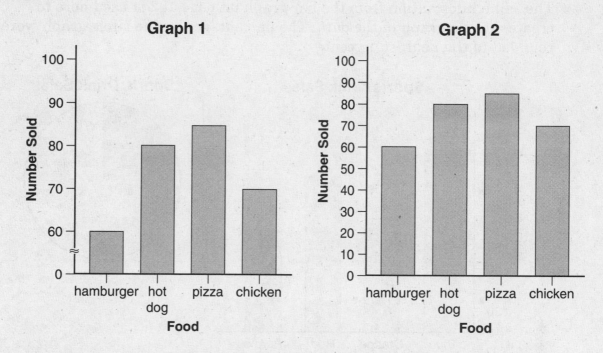

1. One parent claimed that Graph 1 proves that the stand sold three times as many hot dogs as hamburgers. Is this argument valid or invalid?

   _____

2. Another parent said that the graphs were made using different data because the bars in Graph 2 were so much taller than the bars on Graph 1. The parent suggested that the results in Graph 1 might not include sales for the entire day. Is this argument valid or invalid?

   _____

3. If both graphs display the same data, why do they look so different?

   _____
   _____
   _____

# Comparing Graphs

Sometimes you can use more than one type of graph to display the same data. You can compare different graphical representations of the same data to find out which one is better to use in a certain situation.

▶ **Example**

The same information from the bar graph on page 182 is used here to create a circle graph of the data. The percentages on the circle graph were rounded to the nearest percent.

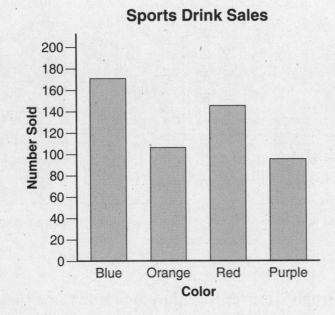

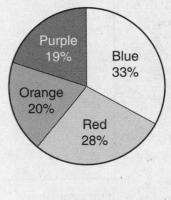

⬤ **Practice**

**Directions:** Use the graphs above to answer Numbers 1 through 3.

1. What percent of the sports drinks sold were blue? _____

2. About how many red sports drinks were sold? _____

3. Explain why you would use each graph in different situations.

_____

_____

_____

# Which Representation Is Best?

The same data can be represented in different ways. Some graphical representations are more appropriate than others for certain kinds of data. Use this table to determine which representation would be best to display different types of data.

## Representations and Purposes

| Representation | Purpose of Data |
|---|---|
| Bar Graph | comparing amounts |
| Histogram | comparing amounts of continuous data |
| Line Graph | showing change over time |
| Circle Graph | comparing parts of a whole |
| Scatterplot | showing relationships between data |

 Practice

**Directions:** For each situation in Numbers 1 through 4, identify the most appropriate representation to display the given data.

1. Show the height of a person at different ages. _____

2. Show how a family budgets their monthly income. _____

3. Show the relationship between number of passes attempted and number of passes completed.

    _____

4. Show total numbers sold for items in the school bookstore.

    _____

5. Which representation would be most appropriate to show the results of an election?

    A. line graph

    B. histogram

    C. circle graph

    D. scatterplot

# Achievement Practice

**Directions: Use the following information to answer Numbers 1 and 2.**

The following list shows the number of unpopped popcorn kernels in 22 bags of microwave popping corn.

25, 28, 32, 39, 41, 42, 47, 51, 54, 55, 66, 68, 69, 70, 71, 72, 74, 76, 77, 79, 80, 82

1. What is the interquartile range of the unpopped kernels?

   A. 74

   B. 57

   C. 42

   D. 32

2. What number of unpopped kernels is at the 70th percentile?

   A. 71

   B. 72

   C. 73

   D. 74

3. Sandy asked her coworkers which player should be MVP for the World Series. Which of the following describes how she selected her sample?

   A. convenience sample

   B. random sample

   C. representative sample

   D. survey response

**Directions: Use the following information to answer Numbers 4 through 6.**

Miss Menosky kept track of the number of students who had to serve a detention each day for one week.

**Student Detentions**

| Day | Number of Students |
|-----------|--------------------|
| Monday | 17 |
| Tuesday | 15 |
| Wednesday | 9 |
| Thursday | 17 |
| Friday | 12 |

4. What is the **median** of the number of students serving detentions?

   A. 9

   B. 12

   C. 15

   D. 16

5. What is the **mean** of the number of students serving detentions?

   A. 15

   B. 14

   C. 13

   D. 12

6. What is the **mode** and the **range** of the number of students serving detentions?

   mode _____

   range _____

7.  The eighth-grade classes of Mr. Scott and Mrs. Salvatori had a contest. They wanted to see which class could bring in more cans of food for the Thanksgiving Day food drive. The results are shown in the following bar graph.

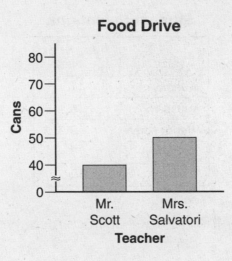

**Food Drive**

Which statement gives the **best** interpretation of the data?

A. Mrs. Salvatori's class brought in double the amount of Mr. Scott's class.

B. Mr. Scott's class brought in ten items more.

C. Mr. Scott's class brought in ten items less.

D. The total number of cans was 100.

8.  For which data set would it **not** be appropriate to use the mean as a measure of central tendency?

A. 15, 74, 80, 19, 81, 68, 22

B. 10, 10, 8, 12, 12, 16, 15

C. 55, 46, 44, 52, 55, 50, 53

D. 22, 21, 19, 27, 25, 30, 24, 26

**Directions: Use the following information to answer Numbers 9 and 10.**

George measured the area of each room in his house. He calculated a total area of 1,600 square feet. He made a circle graph based on the percentage of the total area each room in the house covers.

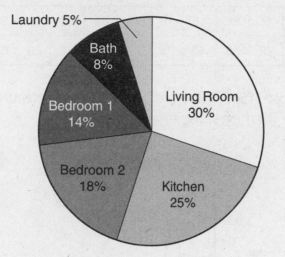

9. What two rooms together account for more than half of the area in the house?

   A. kitchen and bath

   B. living room and bedroom 2

   C. bedroom 2 and bedroom 1

   D. living room and kitchen

10. What is the area of the living room?

   A. 400 square feet

   B. 480 square feet

   C. 520 square feet

   D. 800 square feet

11. The following table shows the relationship between the number of e-mails sent versus the number of e-mails received for 12 employees in a single day.

**Electronic Mail**

| Sent | 5 | 25 | 16 | 10 | 40 | 38 | 40 | 10 | 26 | 35 | 12 |
|---|---|---|---|---|---|---|---|---|---|---|---|
| Received | 22 | 43 | 40 | 35 | 77 | 60 | 82 | 29 | 65 | 57 | 33 |

Use the values from the table to construct a scatterplot of the data. Then draw a trend line that best represents the data.

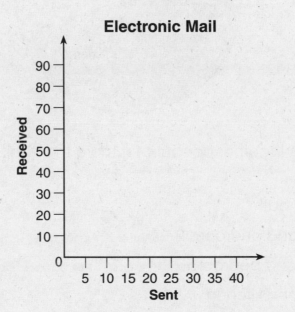

What type of correlation does the scatterplot represent? _____

If an employee sends 50 e-mails in a single day, how many e-mails do you predict that employee will receive?

_____

# Lesson 14: Probability

In this lesson, you will find the probability of simple events and compound events. You will also use counting techniques to calculate the number of possible outcomes for a situation.

## Theoretical Probability

**Theoretical probability** is based on mathematical reasoning. The following formula can be used to find the probability, $P$, that an event will occur.

$$P(\text{event}) = \frac{\text{number of favorable outcomes}}{\text{number of possible outcomes}}$$

Probability can be expressed as a fraction between and including 0 and 1. If an event is certain to occur, its probability is 1. If it is impossible for an event to occur, its probability is 0.

## Simple events

In **simple events**, there is only one outcome.

▷ Example

What is the probability of rolling a 3 on a number cube numbered 1 through 6?

A cube has 6 sides. Each side has a different number on it: 1, 2, 3, 4, 5, or 6. Therefore, the number of possible outcomes is 6. Since each number has an equal chance of being rolled, there is 1 favorable outcome (rolling a 3). The probability is found as follows.

$$P(\text{rolling a 3}) = \frac{\text{number of favorable outcomes}}{\text{number of possible outcomes}} = \frac{1}{6}$$

The probability of rolling a 3 on a number cube is $\frac{1}{6}$.

◆ **TIP:** When probability is expressed as a fraction, it is usually in simplest form.

# ● Practice

**Directions:** For Numbers 1 and 2, fill in the blank to complete the sentence.

1. The probability of an event can be no greater than _____.

2. The probability of an event can be no smaller than _____.

3. If you toss a coin, what is the probability of it landing tails up?

   _____

4. There are 26 red cards in a standard deck of playing cards. If you take those cards and shuffle them, what is the probability of drawing the two of hearts?

   _____

   What is the probability of drawing the two of clubs? _____

**Directions:** Use the following information to find the probabilities for Numbers 5 through 10.

Genny has 36 marbles in a pouch: 9 red, 18 yellow, 1 black, and 8 blue. She is going to take one marble out of the bag without looking.

5. $P$(yellow) _____

6. $P$(red) _____

7. $P$(black) _____

8. $P$(blue) _____

9. $P$(not black) _____

10. What is the best prediction for the color of marble that Genny will take out of her pouch?

    A. yellow

    B. red

    C. black

    D. blue

## Compound events

**Compound events** involve two or more simple events. Compound events involve the use of the words *and* and *or*.

### Independent and dependent events

Two or more events that **are not** influenced by each other are **independent**. Two or more events that **are** influenced by each other are **dependent**. To find the probability of independent or dependent events A **and** B, multiply the probability of the first event by the probability of the second event. Use the following formula.

$$P(\text{A and B}) = P(\text{A}) \cdot P(\text{B})$$

▷ Example

Beth has 8 shirts: 3 white, 2 pink, 1 red, and 2 blue. She has 4 pairs of slacks: 2 black, 1 white, and 1 tan. If Beth takes one shirt and one pair of slacks from her closet without looking, what is the probability that she will select a pink shirt **and** a black pair of slacks?

Since the shirt Beth selects is not influenced by the slacks she picks, the events are independent. Find the probability of each event.

$$P(\text{pink shirt}) = \frac{2}{8} = \frac{1}{4} \qquad\qquad P(\text{black slacks}) = \frac{2}{4} = \frac{1}{2}$$

Multiply the probability of one event by the probability of the other event.

$$P(\text{pink shirt and black slacks}) = P(\text{pink shirt}) \cdot P(\text{black slacks})$$

$$= \frac{1}{4} \cdot \frac{1}{2}$$

$$= \frac{1}{8}$$

The probability that Beth will select a pink shirt and a black pair of slacks is $\frac{1}{8}$.

▷ **Example**

There are 10 pens in a box: 3 red and 7 blue. Two are selected at random and removed. What is the probability of selecting a blue pen first and a red pen second?

Since the second pen selected is influenced by the first pen selected, the events are dependent. Find the probability of each event.

$$P(\text{blue}) = \frac{7}{10} \qquad\qquad\qquad P(\text{red}) = \frac{3}{9} = \frac{1}{3}$$

Multiply the probabilities.

$$P(\text{blue then red}) = P(\text{blue}) \bullet P(\text{red})$$

$$= \frac{7}{10} \bullet \frac{1}{3} = \frac{7}{30}$$

The probability of selecting a blue pen first and a red pen second is $\frac{7}{30}$.

## Mutually exclusive (disjoint) events

Two or more events that cannot happen at the same time are **mutually exclusive**. To find the probability of an event A **or** B in which A and B **cannot** both occur at the same time, find the sum of each probability. Use the following formula.

**$P$(A or B) = $P$(A) + $P$(B)**

▷ **Example**

Jake has a spinner divided into 5 sections of equal size; each section is a different color. The colors on the spinner are red, green, blue, yellow, and orange. What is the probability that Jake's first spin will land on either blue or orange?

Since spinning blue and orange cannot happen at the same time, the events are mutually exclusive. Find the probability of each event.

$$P(\text{blue}) = \frac{1}{5} \qquad\qquad\qquad P(\text{orange}) = \frac{1}{5}$$

Add the probabilities.

$$P(\text{blue or orange}) = P(\text{blue}) + P(\text{orange})$$

$$= \frac{1}{5} + \frac{1}{5} = \frac{2}{5}$$

The probability of spinning either blue or orange is $\frac{2}{5}$.

## ◯ Practice

**Directions:** Use the following information to answer Numbers 1 through 3. Then, write whether the events are *independent*, *dependent*, or *mutually exclusive*.

Stephanie has 30 tulip bulbs to plant: 15 red, 10 purple, and 5 white. She also has 25 iris bulbs to plant: 10 orange and 15 yellow.

1. If Stephanie picks one tulip bulb, what is the probability that it will be either purple **or** white?

   _____

2. If Stephanie picks one tulip bulb and one iris bulb, what is the probability of picking a red tulip bulb **and** a yellow iris bulb?

   _____

3. If Stephanie picks two iris bulbs without replacement, what is the probability of picking an orange bulb first **and** a yellow bulb second?

   _____

4. If two 8-sided number dice, each numbered 1 through 8, are rolled, what is the probability of getting a 3 on each die?

   _____

5. If you roll a 6-sided number cube, what is the probability of rolling an even number?

   _____

6. Grace has a bowl of 27 green and 18 red grapes, mixed. If she takes two grapes from the bowl without replacement, what is the probability that the first grape will be green **and** the second grape will be red?

   _____

7. Suzanne knew that there would be a fire drill 15 minutes after the hour between 9:00 A.M. and noon one school day during the next 4 weeks of school. She took a guess of which day and which time. What is the probability that Suzanne guessed the day **and** time of day correctly?

   _____

# Counting Techniques

You can use different counting techniques to determine the number of possible outcomes for a situation. You can also use counting techniques to determine how many ordered arrangements or combinations you can make from the elements in a given set.

## Fundamental Counting Principle

The **Fundamental Counting Principle (FCP)** is used to find the total number of outcomes when a task consists of several separate parts. Multiply each part together to get the total number of outcomes.

▷ **Example**

> For lunch, Ted can make a sandwich from a choice of 3 types of bread, 4 types of lunch meat, and 2 types of mustard. Use the FCP to determine the number of different sandwiches he can make using one type of bread, one type of lunch meat, and one type of mustard for each sandwich.
>
> $$3 \quad \bullet \quad 4 \quad \bullet \quad 2 \quad = \quad 24 \text{ total outcomes}$$
> $$\uparrow \qquad \uparrow \qquad \uparrow$$
> $$\textbf{bread} \quad \textbf{meat} \quad \textbf{mustard}$$
>
> Ted can make one of 24 different sandwiches.

◯ **Practice**

**Directions:** Use the fundamental counting principle to answer Numbers 1 through 3.

1. How many five-digit even numbers can be created using the digits 0 through 9, with repetition allowed?

   _____

2. The student council is having an election. Five students are running for President, 3 students are running for Secretary, and 2 students are running for Treasurer. How many different groups of 3 newly-elected officers are possible from these choices?

   _____

3. In some states, a license plate has 2 letters followed by 4 digits. How many different license plates are possible? Repetition of digits and letters is allowed.

   _____

# Permutations

**Permutations** are ordered arrangements of the elements from a set.

▷ **Example**

You can use the fundamental counting principle to determine that there are 24 permutations for the letters $a$, $b$, $c$, and $d$ using all four letters ($4 \bullet 3 \bullet 2 \bullet 1 = 24$). How many permutations are there of the four letters using three letters at a time?

| | | | | | |
|---|---|---|---|---|---|
| *abc* | *abd* | *acb* | *acd* | *adb* | *adc* |
| *bac* | *bad* | *bca* | *bcd* | *bda* | *bdc* |
| *cab* | *cad* | *cba* | *cbd* | *cda* | *cdb* |
| *dab* | *dac* | *dba* | *dbc* | *dca* | *dcb* |

Even though only three letters are being used in each permutation, there are still four letters to choose from. Therefore, there are 4 choices for the first letter, 3 for the second, and 2 for the third. There are $4 \bullet 3 \bullet 2 = 24$ permutations.

▷ **Example**

How many permutations are there of the four letters $a$, $b$, $c$, and $d$ using two letters at a time?

| | | | | | |
|---|---|---|---|---|---|
| *ab* | *ac* | *ad* | *ba* | *bc* | *bd* |
| *ca* | *cb* | *cd* | *da* | *db* | *dc* |

There are 4 choices for the first letter and 3 for the second. There are $4 \bullet 3 = 12$ permutations.

▷ **Example**

How many permutations are there of the four letters $a$, $b$, $c$, and $d$ using one letter at a time?

| | | | |
|---|---|---|---|
| *a* | *b* | *c* | *d* |

There are 4 choices for the first and only letter. There are 4 permutations.

The following symbol represents the number of permutations of $n$ elements taken $r$ at a time.

$$_nP_r$$

The number of permutations of 4 elements taken 4 at a time, $_4P_4 = 4 \bullet 3 \bullet 2 \bullet 1$, is a product of four factors.

The number of permutations of 4 elements taken 3 at a time, $_4P_3 = 4 \bullet 3 \bullet 2$, is a product of three factors.

The number of permutations of 4 elements taken 2 at a time, $_4P_2 = 4 \bullet 3$, is a product of two factors.

The number of permutations of 4 elements taken 1 at a time, $_4P_1 = 4$, is the number of elements in the set.

Use the following formula to find the number of permutations of $n$ elements taken $r$ at a time.

$$_nP_r = \frac{n!}{(n-r)!}$$

The formula uses **factorial notation (!)**. Factorial notation means you find the product of all the positive integers less than or equal to the starting integer. For example, $4! = 4 \bullet 3 \bullet 2 \bullet 1 = 24$.

## ▷ Example

Find $_6P_2$, $_9P_4$, and $_{10}P_7$.

$$_6P_2 = \frac{6!}{(6-2)!} = \frac{6!}{4!} = \frac{6 \bullet 5 \bullet 4 \bullet 3 \bullet 2 \bullet 1}{4 \bullet 3 \bullet 2 \bullet 1} = 30$$

$$_9P_4 = \frac{9!}{(9-4)!} = \frac{9!}{5!} = \frac{9 \bullet 8 \bullet 7 \bullet 6 \bullet 5 \bullet 4 \bullet 3 \bullet 2 \bullet 1}{5 \bullet 4 \bullet 3 \bullet 2 \bullet 1} = 3,024$$

$$_{10}P_7 = \frac{10!}{(10-7)!} = \frac{10!}{3!} = \frac{10 \bullet 9 \bullet 8 \bullet 7 \bullet 6 \bullet 5 \bullet 4 \bullet 3 \bullet 2 \bullet 1}{3 \bullet 2 \bullet 1} = 604,800$$

◆ **TIP:** $0! = 1$

## Distinguishable permutations

There are times when you will find duplicate permutations of the elements from a set.

▷ Example

How many permutations are there of the letters *p*, *o*, and *p*?

***pop***    ***ppo***    ***opp***    *opp*    *pop*    *ppo*

There are 3! = 6 permutations, but some of them are the same. There are only 3 **distinguishable permutations**.

▷ Example

How many permutations are there for a 4-digit number using the digits 2, 2, 5, and 9? How many of them are distinguishable?

| | | | | | |
|---|---|---|---|---|---|
| **2,259** | **2,295** | **2,529** | **2,592** | **2,925** | **2,952** |
| 2,259 | 2,295 | 2,529 | 2,592 | 2,925 | 2,952 |
| **5,229** | **5,292** | 5,229 | 5,292 | **5,922** | 5,922 |
| **9,225** | **9,252** | 9,225 | 9,252 | **9,522** | 9,522 |

There are 4! = 24 permutations, of which 12 are distinguishable.

Notice that the distinguishable permutations in each example are half of the total number of permutations. This is due to the fact that there are 2! = 2 permutations of the same element. Notice that there are pairs of permutations that are the same. If 3 elements were the same, then there would be 3! = 6 permutations of the same element. In this case, you would divide the total number of permutations by 6 to find the number of distinguishable permutations.

A similar relationship holds true if one set contains multiple elements that are the same. If there are 2 elements of one kind and 3 elements of another kind, then you divide the total permutations by 2!3! = 12 to find the number of distinguishable permutations.

Use the following formula to find the number of distinguishable permutations of $n$ elements taken $n$ at a time, with $n_1$ elements alike, $n_2$ of another kind alike, and so on.

$$\frac{n!}{n_1!n_2!\ldots}$$

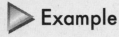 Example

How many distinguishable permutations can be made from the letters in the word INDEPENDENT?

There are 11 letters in the word INDEPENDENT, so there are 11 elements in the set. There are 3 N's, 2 D's, and 3 E's.

Substitute these values into the formula and solve.

$$\frac{11!}{3!2!3!} = \frac{39,916,800}{6 \cdot 2 \cdot 6}$$

$$= \frac{39,916,800}{72}$$

$$= 554,400$$

There are 554,400 distinguishable permutations from the letters in INDEPENDENT.

Example

A pet store has 3 blue dog collars, 4 red dog collars, 1 green dog collar, and 2 yellow dog collars. How many distinguishable ways are there to sell these dog collars one at a time?

Substitute these values into the formula and solve.

$$\frac{10!}{3!4!1!2!} = \frac{3,628,800}{288}$$

$$= 12,600$$

There are 12,600 distinguishable ways to sell the dog collars one at a time.

### ⬤ Practice

**Directions:** For Numbers 1 through 6, find the number of permutations.

1. $_7P_6$

2. $_9P_2$

3. $_{12}P_3$

4. $_6P_3$

5. $_5P_5$

6. $_9P_1$

**Directions:** For Numbers 7 through 12, find the number of distinguishable permutations of all the letters in the following words.

7. TOLEDO

8. CLEVELAND

9. BUCKEYE

10. ALGEBRA

11. ADDITION

12. MISSISSIPPI

**Directions:** For Numbers 13 through 16, find the number of permutations.

13. Joe has to remember a four-digit number code to unlock a door. He remembers that there are two 1's and two 3's. How many distinguishable codes can Joe choose from?

_____

14. There are two summer jobs at the ice cream parlor; 8 students have applied. How many ways are there to fill the two positions?

_____

15. Fifteen people are participating in a math contest. Prizes will be awarded for first, second, and third place finishers. How many ways can the contestants place first, second, and third?

_____

16. There are 8 cups to hang on cup hooks that are arranged in a line. There are 2 blue cups, 3 red cups, 2 green cups, and 1 white cup. How many distinguishable ways can all 8 cups be arranged on the cup hooks?

    A. 40,320

    B. 10,080

    C.  3,360

    D.  1,680

# Combinations

A **combination** is a grouping of the elements from a set in which the order doesn't matter. This means that *abc* and *acb* would be considered the same since all that matters are the elements of the group and not the order in which they appear.

▷ **Example**

How many combinations are there of the four letters *a*, *b*, *c*, and *d* using all four letters?

*abcd*

There is 1 combination.

▷ **Example**

How many combinations are there of the four letters *a*, *b*, *c*, and *d* using three letters at a time?

*abc*     *abd*     *acd*     *bcd*

There are 4 combinations.

▷ **Example**

How many combinations are there of the four letters *a*, *b*, *c*, and *d* using two letters at a time?

*ab*     *ac*     *ad*     *bc*     *bd*     *cd*

There are 6 combinations.

▷ **Example**

How many combinations are there of the four letters *a*, *b*, *c*, and *d* using one letter at a time?

*a*     *b*     *c*     *d*

There are 4 combinations.

The following symbol represents the number of combinations of $n$ elements taken $r$ at a time.

$$_nC_r$$

Use the following formula to find the number of combinations of $n$ elements taken $r$ at a time.

$$_nC_r = \frac{n!}{r!(n-r)!}$$

▷ **Example**

Find $_6C_2$, $_9C_4$, and $_{10}C_7$.

$$_6C_2 = \frac{6!}{2!(6-2)!} = \frac{6!}{2!4!} = \frac{6 \cdot 5 \cdot 4 \cdot 3 \cdot 2 \cdot 1}{2 \cdot 1 \cdot 4 \cdot 3 \cdot 2 \cdot 1} = 15$$

$$_9C_4 = \frac{9!}{4!(9-4)!} = \frac{9!}{4!5!} = \frac{9 \cdot 8 \cdot 7 \cdot 6 \cdot 5 \cdot 4 \cdot 3 \cdot 2 \cdot 1}{4 \cdot 3 \cdot 2 \cdot 1 \cdot 5 \cdot 4 \cdot 3 \cdot 2 \cdot 1} = 126$$

$$_{10}C_7 = \frac{10!}{7!(10-7)!} = \frac{10!}{7!3!} = \frac{10 \cdot 9 \cdot 8 \cdot 7 \cdot 6 \cdot 5 \cdot 4 \cdot 3 \cdot 2 \cdot 1}{7 \cdot 6 \cdot 5 \cdot 4 \cdot 3 \cdot 2 \cdot 1 \cdot 3 \cdot 2 \cdot 1} = 120$$

Compare the number of combinations in each example above with the number of permutations in each of their corresponding examples on page 210.

$_6P_2 = 30$        $_6C_2 = 15$

$_9P_4 = 3{,}024$       $_9C_4 = 126$

$_{10}P_7 = 604{,}800$     $_{10}C_7 = 120$

If you study the rows, you will see that if you take the permutation value and divide it by the factorial of the number taken from the set ($r$), you get the combination value.

$$\frac{30}{2!} = 15$$

$$\frac{3{,}024}{4!} = 126$$

$$\frac{604{,}800}{7!} = 120$$

## ⬤ Practice

**Directions:** For Numbers 1 through 6, find the number of combinations.

1. $_{13}C_3$

2. $_6C_2$

3. $_{10}C_4$

4. $_{10}C_8$

5. $_5C_1$

6. $_{12}C_{11}$

**Directions:** For Numbers 7 and 8, find the number of combinations.

7. Trevor went to a restaurant. He could order 2 side dishes with his dinner from a list of 9 choices. How many different ways can Trevor choose 2 different side dishes from the choices?

_____

8. There are 4 rides at the fair grounds. Jane can choose to ride 2 of them before it is time to go home. How many different ways can Jane choose her rides?

   A. 24

   B. 18

   C. 12

   D. 6

# Achievement Practice

1. Bill will toss a coin and roll a number cube once. What is the probability that the coin will show tails and the number cube will show a multiple of three?

   A. $\frac{1}{2}$

   B. $\frac{1}{3}$

   C. $\frac{1}{6}$

   D. $\frac{5}{6}$

2. How many **distinguishable permutations** can be formed using all the letters in the word GRASSHOPPERS?

   A.  479,001,600

   B.  79,833,600

   C.  39,916,800

   D.  19,958,400

3. Marcie has a collection of 9 DVDs. She will choose 3 of them to take in the car to watch during a long trip. How many combinations of three DVDs can Marcie take from her collection?

   A.  504

   B.  252

   C.  168

   D.  84

4. The football team is drawing names for one pair of cocaptains. There are 5 players from the offensive line and 5 from the defensive line who have their names in the drawing for cocaptain. What is the probability that one player from the offense and one player from the defense will be chosen?

    A. $\frac{1}{25}$

    B. $\frac{1}{20}$

    C. $\frac{1}{10}$

    D. $\frac{1}{5}$

5. In how many ways can Mrs. Hart arrange 6 books on a shelf?

    A. 12

    B. 24

    C. 120

    D. 720

6. At Little Joe's Pizza, there are choices of the following toppings: pepperoni, sausage, onion, peppers, mushrooms, black olives, and anchovies. How many different ways can you order a pizza using any 3 of these toppings?

    A. 960

    B. 240

    C. 42

    D. 35

**Directions: Use the following information to answer Numbers 7 through 9.**

Twenty socks are in a drawer: 6 brown, 8 white, and 6 blue. Socks will be chosen from the drawer without looking.

7.  What is the probability of choosing a sock that is white or blue?

    A.  $\frac{3}{10}$

    B.  $\frac{2}{5}$

    C.  $\frac{7}{20}$

    D.  $\frac{7}{10}$

8.  If two socks are chosen one at a time without replacement, what is the probability of choosing a pair of brown socks?

    A.  $\frac{3}{10}$

    B.  $\frac{3}{5}$

    C.  $\frac{3}{38}$

    D.  $\frac{2}{20}$

9.  If two socks are chosen at the same time, what is the probability of choosing one white sock and one blue sock?

    A.  $\frac{3}{25}$

    B.  $\frac{12}{95}$

    C.  $\frac{7}{190}$

    D.  $\frac{14}{39}$